GRAVE TALES
OF SOUTH YORKSHIRE

Grave Tales

of

South Yorkshire

BY GILES BREARLEY
WITH BRIAN ELLIOTT

Wharncliffe Books

First Published in 2000 by
Wharncliffe Books
an imprint of
Pen and Sword Books Limited,
47 Church Street, Barnsley,
South Yorkshire, S70 2AS

For up-to-date information on other titles produced under the
Wharncliffe imprint, please telephone or write to:

> **Wharncliffe Books**
> **FREEPOST**
> **47 Church Street**
> **Barnsley**
> **South Yorkshire S70 2BR**
> **Telephone (24 hours): 01226 - 734555**

ISBN: 1-871647-70-3

A CIP catalogue record of this book is available from the
British Library

Cover illustration: Wentworth Old Church in Winter *Brian Elliott*

Printed in Great Britain by
Redwood Books, Trowbridge, Wiltshire

CONTENTS

I

THE BARNSLEY AREA

II

THE DONCASTER AREA

III

THE ROTHERHAM AREA

IV

THE SHEFFIELD AREA

INTRODUCTION

by Brian Elliott

Anyone compiling a bibliography on churches as buildings of interest has a vast number of publications to consider. There are also a number of publications on church epitaphs. Unfortunately there are far fewer books available that help us to appreciate the PEOPLE and EVENTS represented on grave-stones in burial places, in other words the stories behind stone inscriptions. A recent book on 'Famous Graves' has only one entry for the whole of South Yorkshire!

Yet for a long time antiquarians and more recently family historians have recognised the importance of monuments and memorials, transcribing and commenting on inscriptions. Such work is extremely valuable as a primary source of information on our recent ancestors. Details carved by stone-masons at the behest of bereaved families can provide us with vital knowledge that might not be available in printed or documentary records. Even the most casual walk through churchyards and cemeteries will reveal fascinating details. They are, despite the unfortunate recent trend of desecration in some of our urban cemeteries, equivalent to open-air museums of the past.

Thankfully, some of our great nineteenth-century cemeteries, though often long neglected, have become increasingly recognised by planning authorities and voluntary organisations as places of considerable importance to present and future generations. Not only do they provide us with a reasonable cross-section of local society but are also havens for wildlife and plants. They also offer considerable artistic and educational potential for children and adults. The movement to establish 'Friends' of cemeteries is certainly a positive and enlightened response in recognising, conserving, campaigning and promoting the value of such places. The National Federation of Cemetery Friends, c/o 42 Chestnut Grove, South Croydon, Surrey CR2 7LH, is a useful address for any one individual, group or organisation interested in cemeteries; and in South Yorkshire the Friends of the [Sheffield] General

Cemetery have done excellent work.

Giles Brearley has visited many South Yorkshire churches, churchyards and cemeteries in his research for this volume. The result is over one hundred examples of gravestones and monuments 'brought to life', providing us with an insight into the lives of a wide range of local individuals, families and tragic events. The choice of what to include has been entirely personal alongside a little advice from the present editor. Hopefully the result will appeal to a wide readership since the subjects cover all members of local society, not just the 'famous' or the wealthy, though some key and sometimes long-forgotten worthies are included. Very many more examples could have been included, indeed a single volume on Sheffield's great General Cemetery alone could have been compiled.

The book has a very wide timespan, from the medieval period to the late twentieth century. More than 250 illustrations have been used to supplement the text which has been arranged in four parts, covering the Barnsley, Doncaster, Rotherham and Sheffield areas.

Every local churchyard and cemetery has some features of interest and access is free to all! Hopefully more popular guides of this kind will become available.

Acknowledgements

The author and editor would like to thank the following individuals and organisations for their kind support when researching and compiling *Grave Tales of South Yorkshire:*

Local Studies' librarians and staff at Barnsley, Doncaster and Rotherham MBC
Doncaster College (High Melton site) library staff
Mexborough Heritage Society
Wombwell Cricket Lovers' Society
Clifton Museum (Rotherham MBC)
Friends of the General Cemetery, Sheffield
Miss N.L. Jackson, Assistant to Registrar, Cole Bros of Sheffield
John Lewis Partnership Archive Collection, Stevenage

The Laird of Camster (Yorks Notes)
Councillor Ken Wyatt
Mrs C. Braithwaite
Graham Oliver
Colin Benton
Gordon Neale
Bryan Dobson
Teresa Danforth
Barry Hirst
Mick Fowler ('drover' painting & photographs)
Alex and Amy Brearley
Mick Pope
Gavin Mackinder, Mark Smallman and Paul Williams (photographs)
Mr P. Warren
Howard Bicknell
Tony Munford
Charles Hewitt, Mike Parsons, Paul Wilkinson, Sylvia Menzies and all
the Wharncliffe team.

ALL ILLUSTRATIONS ARE FROM THE COLLECTION OF GILES BREARLEY
UNLESS OTHERWISE STATED IN CAPTIONS.

I THE BARNSLEY AREA

The Barnsley cemetery, consecrated by the Bishop of Ripon on
6 November 1861, cost nearly £11,000. It has two chapels.
Both are early decorated, and each has a spire. A wall
pierced with arches is built between the two.
The ground has many burials in it, and it is now
studded with head stones. It consists of thirteen acres
of land well laid out, and is a place to which the
inhabitants come in great numbers on Sundays

From: *Walks in Yorkshire: Wakefield and its Neighbourhood*
by W.S. Banks, 1871

Figure 1.1. An early engraving of Barnsley Cemetery. Perkins and Backhouse of Leeds succeeded in gaining the commission for the design of the chapels etc. in a 'contest' involving a total of thirty-seven submissions.
Brian Elliott

Figures 1.2. & 1.3. Thirty years separate these two photographs, Figure 1.2 shows the monument in 1969 and Figure 1.3 in 1999. *Brian Elliott*

Figure 1.4. Detail of the monument inscription.

ARDSLEY, CHRIST CHURCH GRAVEYARD
Oaks Colliery Monument: Christ Church Graveyard

An obelisk marks the site of a mass grave in Ardsley churchyard containing the bodies of thirty-five miners who lost their lives when the nearby Oaks pit 'exploded' like a great spurting volcano on 12 and 13 December 1866 (Figures 1.2 and 1.3). As can be seen in Figure 1.4, it was erected 'BY PUBLIC SUBSCRIPTION' in respect of the 334 'MEN AND BOYS' who were killed. At a time when rescue operations consisted of a mixture of knowledge, goodwill, enthusiasm, desperation and courage rather than practised organisation, some twenty-seven rescue workers were also killed. It remains as one of England's worst industrial disasters.

An inscription on the monument is typical of the great uncertainties of Victorian working class life:

Watch therefore for ye
know neither the day
Nor the hour whenever
The Son of Man Cometh

and

Boast not thyself of
Tomorrow for thou
Knowest not what a
Day may bring forth

Ardsley was one of the two relatively new parishes (the other was Monk Bretton) where interments had been taking place (many of the deceased from Hoyle Mill), along with the recently opened Barnsley cemetery. 'Wailings and lamentations' were reported on the occasion of the mass burial in a grave said to be twelve feet deep and twelve feet square. Coffins were laid lengthways and two abreast. The Reverend Cooke of Darfield and theReverend Micklethwaite of Ardsley 'presided' on this dreadful occasion.

Oaks Obelisk Monument

Ardsley and Monk Bretton parish registers show that bodies were still being recovered from the pit during 1870 and 1871, almost five years after the disaster. From Ardsley alone about fifty-three bodies were left entombed in the stricken workings. The majority of those buried at Ardsley (in the mass

Figure 1.5. The 'Oaks Monument' was erected in 1913, funded by local business man Samuel Joshua Cooper . This postcard was published by Haigh Bros. of Barnsley and posted from Barnsley on 25 February 1919.

OAKS MONUMENT, NR. BARNSLEY,

Figure 1.6. Scene showing the second explosion as shown in the *Illustrated London News*.

and family graves) were under the age of thirty, including four boys aged twelve to fourteen.

When visited by Brian Elliott in 1969 the obelisk, enclosed by a low chain fence of iron, was both leaning and 'blackened' with atmospheric pollution. Subsequent restoration work has now given the monument an air of dignity, though it deserves wider acknowledgement.

The so-called Oaks Monument (another obelisk, see Figure 1.5) on Kendray Hill, even more recently restored, due to insane vandalism, was not erected until 1913, almost sixty years after the disaster had occurred, to commemorate the death of mining engineer Parkin Jeffcock, one of the leaders of the main and ill-fated rescue attempt and the bravery of John Mammatt and Thomas Embleton

Figure 1.7. Edwardian postcard (by George Washington Irving) of Barnsley Main and the old Oaks Colliery pithead (arrowed).

who, after the explosions, descended the pit to bring out 'the sole survivor', Samuel Brown who became something of a local celebrity afterwards. Thus, despite the 'golden angel' on Kendray Hill, the Ardsley monument is in many respects the most appropriate tribute to the Oaks miners and their families.

The *Illustrated London News* published a series of engravings about the disaster (Figure 1.6) and there are a number of postcards of Barnsley Main Colliery which show the old pithead of the Oaks Colliery (Figure 1.7).

BARNSLEY
St Mary's Church and Churchyard

A number of interesting monuments are still extant inside St Mary's Church despite the major rebuilding by Rickman in the early 1820s. Although not entirely a 'Who's-Who' of local worthies, some of the town's 'more important' entrepreneurs and business families are commemorated.

Among them are the Becketts, the well-known benefactors. A classical but relatively plain memorial (Figure 1.8) is in respect of Joseph Beckett, the pioneering merchant and banker (1751-1840), sometimes referred to as 'the father of the Barnsley linen trade' whilst a brass plaque (Figure 1.9) is a tribute to John Staniforth Beckett (1799-1868) who founded the Beckett Dispensary (hospital) and the '[east] window over the altar of this church'. Placed there in 1870 it concludes

Figure 1.8. Monument to Joseph Beckett. *Brian Elliott*

Figure 1.9. Brass relating to John Staniforth Beckett. *Brian Elliott*

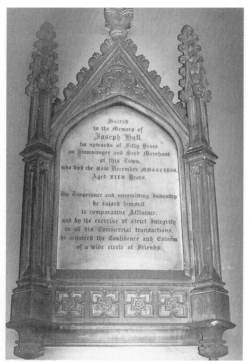

Figure 1.10. Monument to Joseph Hall
Brian Elliott

with the phrase, *'O Lord in Thee have I trusted let me never be confounded'*.

Another, more ornate example (Figure 1.10) is to Joseph Hall, described as 'for over fifty years an Ironmonger and Seed merchant'. The inscription is a delightful example of mid-Victorian ethic and complimentary monumental language, referring to the deceased's hard-working and sober attributes and his 'strict integrity in all commercial transactions...', which gained 'the confidence and esteem of a wide circle of friends'. Hall's premises were near the bottom of Market Hill on a site adjacent to the present NatWest Bank.

The old churchyard and now its landscaped extension (Figure 1.11) contain many interesting gravestones of local families (Figures 1.12-17) of more modest social standing but they are particularly interesting for their occupational

Figure 1.11. St Mary's Church and landscaped churchyard extension. *Brian Elliott*

Figure 1.12. This is one of the eighteenth-century gravestones relating to William Burgess, a Barnsley joiner, who died 'in the 28th year of his age', in 1764 and his son, Jonathan, sugar-refiner who died thirteen years later. *Brian Elliott*

Figure 1.13. Richard Travis, who died aged twenty-nine in 1795 was a hat-maker by trade and business as can be seen by reference to this monumental inscription. Travis' widow, Ellen, lost her two year eleven month old son, David, just three days after her husband's death. Further family deaths are also recorded up to 1870. *Brian Elliott*

information, often supplementing parish register information, and therefore of considerable importance to the family and local historian

> *My dust lies here as you may see*
> *I've left no child to weep for me*
> *A wife sincere I left to mourn*
> *But soon she must to dust return.*
> Brian Elliott

Figure 1.14. William Truelove (c.1740-1810) was a 'cordwainer' [shoemaker], a common Barnsley trade as we can see from this gravestone. Interestingly, we can also see that his son, John, was killed in the Crimean War, in 1855. *Brian Elliott*

Figure 1.15 (left). William Hammerton (c.1756-1821) is referred to as a 'wire manufacturer' on his gravestone. Wire-making was once the staple trade of Barnsley.

Figure 1.16 (below). Joshua Wilkinson has the somewhat unusual occupational title of 'Music-Seller' on his family gravestone, where his wife and son are interred. *Brian Elliott*

Figure 1.17 (above). There are a number of 'Druggist' gravestones. Here we have young George Wilson, who died in the year of Waterloo (1815), aged twenty-one. *Brian Elliott*

BARNSLEY CEMETERY

John Smith 1830–66, mining engineer

One of the more prominent monuments in Barnsley cemetery is to the memory of John Smith who was an under-viewer (mining engineer and manager) at Lundhill Colliery (Figure 1.18). Smith, aged thirty-six, was one of the twenty-six volunteer rescue workers killed at the Oaks Colliery as a consequence of the second great explosion that occurred there on 13 December 1866. His body was not recovered until 9 November 1868. The obelisk was 'erected by a few friends who deeply regret his loss'. John Smith's widow lived for a further fifty years, and died, aged eighty-five, in 1916.

The Public Hall Disaster 1908

Another black day in Barnsley's history occurred on Saturday 11 January 1908 when sixteen children, aged between four and eight met their deaths through suffocation at a cinematograph presentation. A further thirteen were injured. The event had been well-publicised, attracting several hundred smiling children. From the top of the gallery landing the presenter, Hugh Rain, instructed incoming children to descend the stairs and enter via the main entrance, not realising that hundreds of others were eagerly rushing up the twisting stone steps. The result was absolute mayhem, a sea of crushing bodies, terrible cries and piercing screams. There was a succession of sad scenes at the cemetery. Many of the children were buried there on the Wednesday. Bands played sombre tunes and there were processions from the Sunday schools, large crowds gathering at the cemetery gates. The event attracted national media coverage. Almost £253 was raised in support of the bereaved

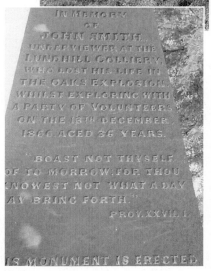

Figures 1.18a and 1.18b Grave obelisk commemorating John Smith, under-viewer at Lundhill Colliery, who lost his life during rescue operations at the Oaks Colliery 13 December 1866. *Brian Elliott 1970 and Giles Brearley 1999*

Figure 1.19. Warner Gothard's hurriedly-produced postcard of the Public Hall disaster, shows thirteen of the sixteen children who died on Saturday 11 January 1908. *Brian Elliott Collection*

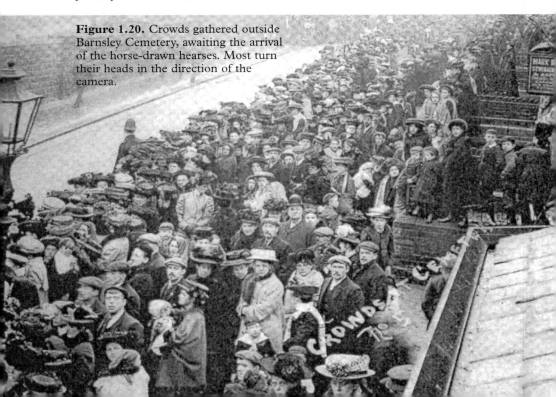

Figure 1.20. Crowds gathered outside Barnsley Cemetery, awaiting the arrival of the horse-drawn hearses. Most turn their heads in the direction of the camera.

families, grants of £10 being allocated to affray funeral costs. A postcard, now a sought after collector's item, was hurriedly created by opportunistic Warner Gothard, showing the stairs, Public Hall, assembled crowd, Beckett Hospital and gallery entrance, along with photographs of thirteen of the children. Gothard must have worked very quickly, borrowing photographs from mourning parents, since this card (Figure 1.19) was sent from Worsbrough on 16 January, only five days after the disaster. A series of other cards was produced showing crowd scenes (Figure 1.20) and horse-drawn hearses.

John Elliott JP 1844-1919, Co-operative pioneer.

From its foundation in 1862 until recent years, 'the Coop' has been a most important part of the lives of residents of Barnsley and its neighbourhood. John Elliott (1844-1919, Figure 1.21) was a director and president of the Barnsley British Cooperative Society 'for thirty-six years'. He had joined the Society in 1869 when there were less than a thousand members, succeeded to a directorship fifteen years later and was elected president in 1899, following the retirement of James Fairclough. As a young man he had served his business 'apprenticeship' with the Clay Cross Iron Company, moving to Wombwell in 1869 to develop further his commercial interests but also he immersed himself in local government and religious affairs. He was a member of the Local Board and Urban District Council, helped found the Band of Hope and Sunday School Unions and for many years served as Superintendent of the Wesleyan Sunday School.

Figure 1.21.
John Elliott,
1844-1919

In 1869 the BBCS consisted of a central grocery in Barnsley and branches at Dodworth, Wombwell, Higham, Warren, Ardsley, Gawber and Penistone. By the end of Elliott's presidency there were branches throughout the Barnsley area. The central premises had expanded so as to include a drapery and departments for tailoring, butchery, boots, groceries and confectionery, fish and game, millinery and dressmaking (Figure 1.22). There was also a mineral water manufacturer, a bakery, cold store and a finance and mortgage department. Elliott introduced policies of education for staff and workers. His memorial (Figure 1.23) can be located by entering the main gate and walking forward

Figure 1.22. 'Birds-Eye view of Central Premises' from The Coronation History of the Barnsley British Co-operative Society Limited 1862-1902 (1903)

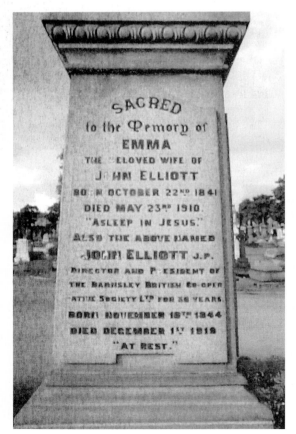

forty yards. It is the second grave on the left-hand side.

Christopher Lindley c1805-64, linen manufacturer

By the early 1800s Barnsley emerged as one of the premier regions for the manufacture of a variety of linen products. Christopher Lindley was one of the less well-known manufacturers. The industry began to decline during the 1850s. One of the last mills associated with the trade, at Redbrook, closed in 1937 (Figure 1.24). Weavers' cottages are still extant at Stafford Walk and High Street, Dodworth;

Figure 1.23. John Elliott's memorial

also at Darton Road, Cawthorne and Top Row, Brierley. Warehouses operated at Dodworth Green and St Mary's Place, the latter continuing until 1882. Town weavers' cottages have of course been demolished (Figure 1.25). Lindley's grave can be seen after entering the main gate, turning left at the centre chapel, after fifty yards look to the right and the grave is the third inwards.

Figure 1.24 (upper photograph). Redbrook Mill
Figure 1.25. Weavers' cottages, Barnsley

Figure 1.26. John Buckley's gravestone

John Buckley c1847-73, bleacher
Bleaching was an essential process in the 'finishing' of linen manufacture. Harold Taylor has shown that by the middle of the nineteenth century bleachworks were located by the Dearne at Swithin (Darton), Redbrook, Greenfoot, Old Mill, Beevor (Oakwell), Hoyle Mill, Newbridge (Monk Bretton), Cudworth (Midland), Stairfoot, Rob Royd (Dodworth) and Ardsley. When John Buckley died at the premature age of twenty-six, on 10 July 1873, the entire linen industry of the town and district was in serious decline. His gravestone (Figure 1.26), which can be seen by turning right before the chapel (for about 100 yards), the 7th grave on the left side, serves as a reminder of a once important Barnsley industry.

Benjamin Gaunt 1835-88, watchmaker and jeweller
Barnsley has a good reputation for its clock and watchmakers, dating back to the seventeenth century when owning a timepiece of any description was a sign of status and wealth. During the Victorian period a number of jewellery and watchmaking businesses had been established in the town. One of the most prominent was that established by Benjamin Gaunt

Figure 1.27. Advert for Gaunt and Sons 1888, the year of Benjamin's death. *Brian Elliott Collection*

What we have said
We have said.
It is true every time we have said it and it is true to-day.

We have the largest, most valuable, and most comprehensive

Watchmakers & Jewellers' Stock
IN SOUTH YORKSHIRE.

We ask you when you are buying anything in our line, to put us in competition.

BENJⁿ. GAUNT & SONS,
THE OLD ESTABLISHED
Watchmakers & Jewellers,
3 & 4. **MAY DAY GREEN,**
BARNSLEY.

Established over 50 Years.   Telephone 169.

from typically distinctive premises at 3-4 May Day Green. Gaunt had served his apprenticeship under Thomas Allen of Queen Street, striking out on his own account in about 1863 on the north side of May Day Green. For a few years in the 1870s Gaunt, a Wesleyan and a freemason, served on the town council as a Conservative. He died at his residence in Huddersfield Road on 16 June 1888, in middle-age, at fifty-three but his two sons had already considerable experience in the family business which continued to prosper (Figures 1.27-30). Gaunt's grave (Figure 1.30a) can be located by walking right at the ruined chapel and continuing towards the wall; it is a hundred yards on the right, 7th grave inwards.

Figure 1.28. A 1914 advert for Gaunt and Sons, now referred to as 'THE OLD ESTABLISHED.' *Brian Elliott Collection*

Figure 1.29. The Benjamin Gaunt shop, May Day Green, from an Edwardian picture postcard. *Brian Elliott Collection*

BENJN. GAUNT & SONS, Watchmakers and
Jewellers, 3 and 4, May Day Green, Barnsley.—In
the central part of May Day Green is the well-known
establishment of Messrs. Benjn. Gaunt and Sons,
who hold the proud distinction of being the
oldest established watchmakers and jewellers in the
district. They are "The" Watchmakers par excellence. It
has long been a place of interest to all the principal inhabitants,
both in and around the town, as the foremost house in the
silversmith's and jewellery trade. The business was founded
and carried on most successfully for a great number of years by
the late Mr. Benjn. Gaunt, who was personally very highly
esteemed by all sections of the community. In the year 1883
he took his two sons (Messrs. T. T. and B. E. Gaunt) into
partnership, the business being carried on under the name of
Benjn. Gaunt and Sons. Both of them have devoted their best
energies and unique experience to the various details of the
business. They have developed the old trade and opened out
new departments, with the very satisfactory results that they
have taken a premier position amongst the tradesmen of the
town, and at the same time received the confidence of their
numerous customers and friends.

Those who have had the pleasure of looking through their
collection of ornaments, clocks, watches, silver and electro-plate,
jewellery, leather goods, and optical instruments in their
establishment will readily see that the greatest care has been
exercised in placing before the public one of the most comprehensive stocks of valuable, useful, and artistic goods that it
is possible to get together. Their stock of silver ware, modern
and antique, is indeed a revelation ; they are enabled to make a
great display of every article that is manufactured in pure silver.

Messrs. Gaunt and Sons have also made a special study of
the eyesight, in fact they are practical opticians. They hold an
immense stock of spectacles and eye-glasses suitable for every
defect of vision, the greatest care being taken to test the eyesight of every customer.

We must not omit to mention that Messrs. Gaunt and Sons
have long been noted for their Presentation Goods, such as
Bowls, Cups, Plate, Clocks, &c.; also for Sport Prizes. They
are prepared to submit samples or prepare special designs
at short notice.

We strongly recommend all visitors to Barnsley to pay
them a visit, as their shops and windows are one of the sights
of the town. We know that Messrs. Gaunt and Sons will
only be too pleased to shew anyone round and explain their
methods of carrying on such a large business. Their only
address is 3 & 4, May Day Green, Barnsley.

Figure 1.30. Description of the
Gaunt business, from *The
Barnsley Annual* of 1897. *Brian
Elliott Collection*

Figure 1.30a. Detail of Gaunt's grave
inscription.

Robert Andrews, c1856-68, soldier

A fine military career came to an
end in a tragic accident, according
to the inscription on Robert
Andrews' grave:

> *Robert, Son of Josiah and
> Sibberia Andrews,
> late of Pershore, Worcestershire.
> He served in the 20th Regiment
> upwards of ten years and was
> Sergeant therein, he received medals
> and bars for services in the Crimean
> War (Figure 1.31) and the Relief of
> Lucknow. After leaving hisRegiment
> and in discharge of duty, he was
> accidentally killed at the Barnsley
> railway station on November 19th
> 1868 aged 32 years.*

From the main gate, proceed to the
chapel, take the next right-hand
path and at left bed proceed
inwards for ten yards, and Robert
Andrews' grave can be located.

Figure 1.31. Troopship about to set sail to the East, August 1857. Wives and families return to shore after leave-taking. From a painting by Henry N. O'Neil.

William Parrott MP 1843-1905, miners' leader

From January to October 1876 William Parrott (Figure 1.32) served as President of the West Yorkshire Miners' Association and, until 1881, as its Assistant Secretary. After the subsequent merger of the West Yorkshire and South Yorkshire Miners' Associations, Parrott worked as agent and, for a short time until his death, as Secretary to the Yorkshire Miners' Union whose

Figure 1.32. William Parrott

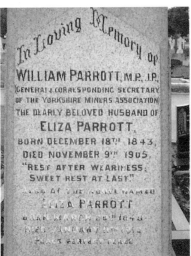

Figure 1.33. The distinctive grave of William Parrott.

new headquarters was in Barnsley. His gravestone can be located from the main gate, fifty yards on the left, second grave down (Figure 1.33).

Robert William Oxley c1868-1909, monumental sculptor

The development of large town cemeteries was understandable locational attraction for monumental masons. The Oxley family business, located on Doncaster Road (Figure 1.34), undertook many

Figure 1.34. Headed paper from a 1967 invoice from F.W. Oxley and Sons Ltd, monumental sculptors.

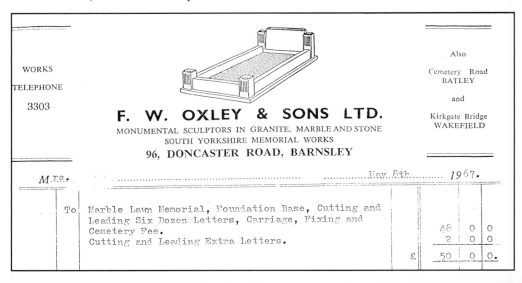

WORKS

TELEPHONE

3303

Also

Cemetery Road
BATLEY

and

Kirkgate Bridge
WAKEFIELD

F. W. OXLEY & SONS LTD.

MONUMENTAL SCULPTORS IN GRANITE, MARBLE AND STONE
SOUTH YORKSHIRE MEMORIAL WORKS
96, DONCASTER ROAD, BARNSLEY

Mrs.   May 8th   1967.

To	Marble Lawn Memorial, Foundation Base, Cutting and Leading Six Dozen Letters, Carriage, Fixing and Cemetery Fee. Cutting and Leading Extra Letters.		48	0	0
			2	0	0
		£	50	0	0.

commissions for families interred in Barnsley cemetery over several generations. A splendid stone cross about seven feet high marks the grave of William Oxley who is described as 'sculptor of this town' who died on 7 January 1909, aged forty-one. His memorial can be seen by passing through the main gate, turning right and proceeding a hundred yards. The grave (Figure 1.35) is on the left of the path.

Undertakers and Mourning Wear

Finally, a word about funeral directors and mourning fashion. There were several private concerns operating in Barnsley during the late Victorian and Edwardian period. They were not slow to advertise their services as can be seen in the following examples (Figures 1.36-1.38). 'Mourning attire' also provided business opportunities for a number of Barnsley retailers, most notably at Butterfields and Baileys where a considerable range of garments could be bought (Figures 1. 39-40).

Figure 1.35. Robert Oxley's grave and memorial.

Figure 1.36. S.C. Collier's 'Funeral Establishment' was based at the Royal Hotel Livery Stables, offering 'Elaborately Carved Hearses With or Without Ostrich Feathers' in 1888. *Brian Elliott Collection*

Figure 1.37. Booker Bros offered mourners 'Glass Sided or Black Carved Hearses' and 'Infants' Mourning Coaches' from the Coach & Horses Hotel in 1888. *Brian Elliott Collection*

Figure 1.38. In 1898 W.L.Rooke & Sons provided a wide range of funeral hearses and carriages pulled by black horses, from the King's Head Hotel Stables. *Brian Elliott Collection*

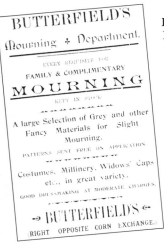

Figure 1.39. Advert for Butterfield's Mourning Department includes references to 'widows' caps' and 'fancy materials for slight mourning', 1898. *Brian Elliott*

Figure 1.40. Edward Bailey of Cheapside had a shop dedicated to selling mourning attire as can be seen in this advertisement of 1898. *Brian Elliott*

BARNSLEY MEETING HOUSE BURIAL GROUND
John Fletcher and Samuel Nickolson - 17th century Quakers.

There have been Quaker communities in and around Barnsley since the founding of the movement in the 1650s when, during a period of great persecution, a burial ground was established at a remote site on Burton Bank, overlooking the Dearne, in Monk Bretton township. Towards the end of the seventeenth century a small meeting house was erected there but a hundred years later it had fallen into disrepair and the main centre of worship was in Barnsley. A new meeting house was built off Huddersfield Road in 1815. A small number of early gravestones, rescued from the abandoned Burton graveyard,

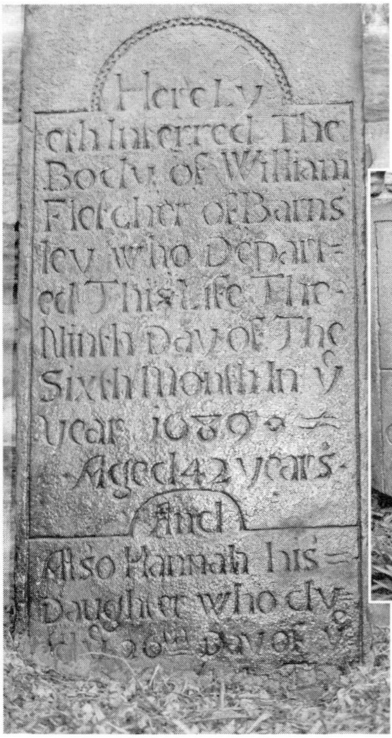

Figure 1.41. Gravestone of William Fletcher. *Brian Elliott*
Figure 1.42. Gravestone of Samuel Nickolson. *Brian Elliott*

can still be seen at Barnsley Meeting House. The gravestone of William Fletcher (Figure 1.41) who died aged forty-two in 1689, is a particularly well-preserved example. The gravestone of Samuel Nickolson (Figure 1.42) 'late of Darton' is crudely carved and probably dates from the same period.

DARFIELD, ALL SAINTS' PARISH CHURCHYARD
Ebenezer Elliott 1781-1849, the 'poor man's poet' and 'corn-law rhymer'.

Elliott was born at Masborough, near Rotherham (Fig.1.43-44) where his father owned an iron foundry. After a brief formal education Ebenezer worked for his father until the age of twenty-three when the 'partnership' floundered through disagreement. The young man had taken to drink. He cured himself by developing a deep interest in botany and nature and father and son became reconciled. He was regarded as a 'difficult' character and in his own writings admitted that 'from my mother I have derived my nervous irritation, my bashful awkwardness, my miserable proneness to anticipate evil, that makes existence all catastrophe'.

Elliott took to the pen and started producing poetry and other works. He was described as writing like a man who was at war with the world. He had a good command of the English language and a good feeling for the beauty of nature. He wrote his first poem, *Vernal Walk*, when he was sixteen and it was published in 1801. Later notable poems included *The Ranter, The Village Patriarch* (1829), *The Corn Law Rhymes* (1831, a bitter condemnation of the 'bread tax') and *The Splendid Village, The People's Anthem* (1847), all so popular that Elliott became a household name and was regarded as 'The Poor Man's Poet'.

Figure 1.43. Ebenezer Elliott

Ebenezer's wealth was

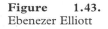

Figure 1.44. Elliott's writing: an autobiographical extract

Figure 1.45. Hargate Hill, near Great Houghton, Elliott's retirement home.

enhanced by an early marriage which enabled him to invest and develop his father's ironworks. But all did not go well, perhaps because of the stormy father-son relationship. In 1821 he started his own bar iron merchant works in Sheffield, a concern that traded successfully, enabling him to retire - in 1842 - in some comfort to a cottage (Figure 1.45) near Great Houghton where he died in 1849, in his 65th year.

Epitaph:

> *Stop mortal! here thy brother lies,*
> *The poet of the poor.*
> *His books were rivers, woods and skies*
> *The meadow and the moor.*
> *His teachers were the torn hearts Wale*
> *The tyrant and the slave,*
> *The street, the factory, the Gaol,*
> *The palace and the grave!*

Elliott's grave (Figures 1.46-48) can be seen a few yards to the south-east of the church tower, protected by a wrought iron fence.

Figure 1.46. Elliott's grave, the tower of All Saints' Church in the background. *Brian Elliott*
Figure 1.47. Elliott's grave, enclosed by an iron fence.
Figure 1.48. Elliott's grave: detail of inscription along the apex of the stone slab. *Brian Elliott*

Lundhill Colliery, 1857 disaster memorial: 'Prepare to Meet Thy God'

One of saddest memorials in any English setting can be seen at the southern edge of Darfield's old churchyard, a grim blackened obelisk commemorating a black day (Figures 1.49-50). On 19 February

Figure 1.49. The Lundhill Colliery disaster memorial. *Brian Elliott*

Figure 1.50. Detail of the Lundhill disaster inscription. *Brian Elliott*

1857 an explosion devastated Lundhill Colliery at a time when 214 men and boys had descended the shaft to begin their mining duties (Figure 1.51). When the rescuers entered the pit their way was impeded in the southern direction because the seam was on fire. They were in danger of losing their own lives and left the mine at once, just before a second explosion sent a fireball up the shaft. Access to the mine could only be gained if the fire was extinguished. A stream was diverted down the shaft to flood the galleries. Some 185 bodies were eventually recovered. The disaster left ninety widows and 220 fatherless children, yet another terrible example of the price of coal.

Figure 1.51. An artist's impression of the second explosion at Lundhill. *Brian Elliott*

Figure 1.52. A drover with a flock of sheep. *Michael Fowler*

Henry Cross c1746–1787, drover

The business of driving sheep and cattle via green lanes to market was a regular activity, long before the development of the American West (Figure 1.52). Many individuals, such as Henry Cross, worked for the yeomen of the area, transporting herds and flocks and managing sales. Animals from Lincolnshire were often driven to the more heavily populated parts of Yorkshire. His gravestone, sited at the end of the church, fourth grave on the right has the following inscription:

> *Here lies the body of Henry Cross*
> *late from Huterby near Luagh*
> *(Lough), Lincolnshire, Drover*
> *and salesman who departed this*
> *life the 30th day of June 1787*
> *aged 41 years.*

Figure 1.53. The gravestone that killed its maker.

Robert Millthorp c1857-1876, mason, killed by a tombstone he was making

Robert Millthorp, a young mason in the employ of a Mr Wraywood of Ardsley, was preparing a memorial when the stone fell and crushed him. The finished memorial (Figure 1.53) was then used as a fitting tribute. The inscription reads:

Here lies the mortal remains of Robert Millthorp
who died 13th September 1876
aged 19 years.
He lost his life by inadvertently throwing this stone
on himself, whilst in the service of
J. Wraywood of Ardsley, who erected it to his memory (alas how frail this brittle clay).

Though form'd with matchless art Death waits in ambush for his prey and none escapes his dart.

A youthful frolic prompted on
While the grave tyrant gave
The mortal strike by this same stone
That makes my early grave.

PENISTONE, ST JOHN'S CHURCHYARD
Nicholas Saunderson 1682-1739, blind mathematician

Nicholas Saunderson (Figure 1.54) was born at New Row, Thurlstone, in 1682. When he was only twelve months old he lost his sight and his eyes after a bad infection of smallpox. Never to be deterred, the youngster is alleged to have learnt letters by passing his fingers over the monumental inscriptions in Penistone churchyard (Figure 1.55), many years before Braille was invented. There is no way of

Figure 1.54. Nicholas Saunderson, Professor of Mathematics.

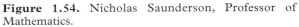

confirming this story, though most people would have had unmarked graves in the late seventeenth century. His great strength was un- doubtedly his memory, his ability to recall information was astounding. Saunderson attended Penistone Grammar School where Mr Staniforth taught him classics, becoming competent in Latin, Greek and French. After school he studied mathematics at home until 1707 when he went to Cambridge – not as a scholar – but as a teacher. Here he taught Newton's optics and became one of the greatest mathematicians of the age, writing a two-volumed treatise, *Algebra*, post- humously published in 1740. He was made MA by special patent and in 1728 elected Lucasian Professor of Mathematics – the most prestigious mathematical job in the country – a title previously held by Isaac Newton. He was created LLD by King George II. Saunderson died of scurvy on 19 April 1739, aged fifty-six, at Toxworth, near Cambridge where there is a monument to his memory. A local memorial can be seen in the small garden opposite Thurlstone post-office.

Figure 1.55. Penistone Church and churchyard. *Brian Elliott*

SILKSTONE, ALL SAINTS' CHURCH AND CHURCHYARD
Thomas Wentworth d.1675, knighted by Charles II

Several generations of the Wentworths of Bretton Hall (Figure 1.56) are interred in All Saints' Church, Silkstone. The magnificent marble monument (by Claudius Rene?) of Sir Thomas Wentworth and his wife, Grace, dating from about 1675, is a large and splendid feature (Figure 1.57-58). Thomas, the third son of George and Mary Wentworth, succeeded his brother in 1641, during the Civil War. A royalist, he served in Scotland and fought at the Battle of Naseby,

Figure 1.56. Bretton Hall, the ancestral home of the Wentworths.

after which he was imprisoned. It was said that Wentworth forfeited £4,000, a very substantial sum, after the Civil War, for his royalist allegiance. A further period of imprisonment – under Cromwell's orders – took place in 1657-58 and Wentworth only just escaped from losing all his estates. After the Restoration, however, his royal support was recognised by King Charles II who bestowed a knighthood and made him a baronet. Towards the end of his life, Wentworth began to lose his sight. He moved to Salisbury in search of medical treatment but died there, in December 1675. Buried in Silkstone Church, his recumbent effigy is accompanied by an outline of his sufferings and achievements. His funeral was probably one of the grandest in the Barnsley area and was said to have attracted some 4,000 mourners.

The Husker Pit Disaster memorial 1838

What has become to be regarded as the Husker Pit memorial can be seen to the west of Silkstone Church, by the churchyard boundary wall (Figures 1.59-61). It marks the grave of twenty-six children and young adults who were killed in a terrible mining disaster. The pit was located off Moorend Lane and a stream ran nearby. The July weather was hot and sultry. A thunderstorm broke out. The rain was so intense that the normally slow running stream became a raging torrent, rapidly flooding the underground workings of the Husker drift mine. The flood waters extinguished the furnace fires which helped to ventilate the pit. Many of the trapped workers were young children. Realising the danger, they tried to escape but the waters

Figure 1.57. The magnificent monument to Sir Thomas Wentworth and his wife, Grace.

Figure.1.58. A detailed view of the two Wentworth effigies shows Grace wearing fashionable dress and Thomas in suitable 'military' attire.

Figure 1.59. 'Boast not thyself of tomorrow': The Husker Pit memorial. *Brian Elliott*

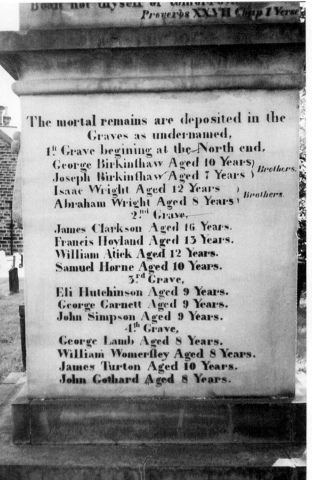

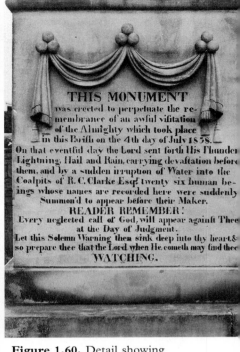

Figure 1.60. Detail showing part of the inscription for some of those buried in four (of seven) graves. *Brian Elliott*

Figure 1.61.
The 'commemorative' part of the monumental inscription with its ominous warning to 'readers'. *Brian Elliott*

burst into the drift and they were drowned. Girls were buried at the boys' feet. The age range was from seven to seventeen years.

WOMBWELL CEMETERY
Roy Kilner 1890-1928, Yorkshire and England cricketer

Roy was born on 17 October, 1890, the second son of Seth and Mary Kilner who lived at Broadbent Cottages, Low Valley, between Wombwell and Darfield. While he was still a baby, Roy's parents moved to Rose Cottage, overlooking the Mitchell Main cricket ground. Seth, originally from Huddersfield, had found employment at Mitchell Main colliery. He had made friends with Irvin Washington, a well-known local sportsman whose sister he was to marry. Washington was a talented batsman who played for Yorkshire between 1900 and 1902.

Roy was encouraged to play cricket at an early age by his father and Uncle Irvin, appearing in the Mitchell Main side at the age of fourteen, in 1905. He played for them over the next four seasons, building on his skills and, by 1909, his reputation had extended beyond Wombwell. On 19 June 1909 he scored his first century for Mitchell Main, sharing a partnership of 215 with his Uncle Irvin. Roy then scored 62 against Rawmarsh, 45 against Hickleton and 68 (not out) versus Wath. In the 1909 season he scored 448 runs at an average of 34.46. The Yorkshire selectors were alerted by the young prospect.

At the end of June 1910 Roy was called up to play for the Yorkshire second eleven in a match against Surrey but, perhaps due to nerves, he was dismissed for nought. His first Yorkshire season was not particularly good, his highest score being only 36 against Staffordshire at Stoke.

Figure 1.62. Roy Kilner, wearing his Yorkshire CC cap and blazer.

In local cricket Roy continued to make good scores which encouraged the Yorkshire board to have a second look at him. He was allocated to Harrogate Cricket Club for the 1911 season where he again demonstrated his true skills with 102 not out against Bradford. His bowling ability emerged, with 7/33 against Skipton. Later in the season Kilner made his debut for the Yorkshire first team at Taunton against Somerset but he was again dismissed without scoring.

In 1912 Sir Archibald White was Yorkshire's captain and he gave Kilner a further opportunity in the match against Nottinghamshire at Trent Bridge. After taking 4 for 66 in Notts' total of 261 he

Figure 1.63. Roy Kilner in action for Yorkshire as a bowler.

was again dismissed for a duck in the first innings. Chasing 249 to win, and with Yorkshire batting at 133 for 4, Kilner and Tasker came together and hit a splendid 103 for the fifth wicket. Tasker made 52 and Kilner a splendid 83 not out. Yorkshire won the match and by the end of the season Roy had amassed 570 runs.

By 1913 Roy was a regular First Xl player for Yorkshire (Figure 1.62). His first century came against Leicestershire, in a partnership of 184 with friend Major Booth. He also scored 104 against Northants. At the end of the season he had accumulated 1,500 runs, including a dozen scores over fifty. Early in season 1914 he scored 169 against Gloucestershire but the outbreak of the First World War brought his cricket to a halt.

Major Booth and Kilner left the Yorkshire squad and enlisted in the Leeds and Bradford battalion of the West Yorkshire Regiment stationed at Colsterdale, but in November 1914 Roy was given special leave to return to Wombwell for his wedding to Annie Campell-John. Major Booth was best man. Kilner went on to see service in Egypt and France where his close friend, Booth, was killed at La Cigney in 1916. Roy was wounded in the same action and sent to Blackpool to convalesce.

When he was fit again he was sent to Preston Garrison to work as a mechanic. While there he played right-back for Preston North End FC.

At the end of the First World War, Roy was able to return to first class cricket for Yorkshire. The side was depleted by the loss of such players as Booth and Alonzo Drake. The county championship of 1919 was not a vintage competition but Yorkshire emerged as champions for the tenth time. During the season Roy scored over 1,000 runs including three centuries. To try to replace the bowling strength that had been lost Kilner was increasingly called upon to develop his skills in that department (Figure 1.63).

In 1920 Roy played in a great needle match against Hampshire at Bramall Lane where he made 206 not out and he took twenty-seven wickets in the season. In 1921 his haul of wickets more than doubled to 61 and he proved to be a true all-rounder in 1923 by scoring 1,198 runs and taking 122 wickets.

Roy Kilner's fame was spreading and he was recognised as one of the best players in the country. In 1924 he was called into the England squad for a series against South Africa but did not play in a match. In the 1924/1925 season he was recalled to play for England on the Australian tour. In the third test at Adelaide he bowled 56, six-ball overs, taking 4 for 127 and then 4 for 57 in the second innings.

SUMMARY

Batting and Fielding

	M.	I.	N.O.	Runs	H.S.	Avge	100s	50s	Cent. P'ships	ct
County Championship	323	416	39	11511	206*	30.53	13	65	42	207
Other Matches for Yorkshire	42	62	7	1507	120	27.40	2	10	6	24
Test Matches	9	8	1	233	74	33.28	—	2	1	6
Other Matches in UK	18	25	3	600	113	27.27	1	2	—	8
Other Matches in Australia	9	14	1	319	103	24.53	1	1	1	3
Other Matches in West Indies	12	15	4	249	54	22.63	—	1	—	17
TOTALS	413	540	55	14419	206*	29.72	17	81	50	265

Bowling

	Overs	Mdns	Runs	Wkts	Avge	5 wkts in Inns	10 wkts in Match	Best in Inns
County Championship	7223.4	2702	12841	784	16.37	39	9	8:26
Other Matches for Yorkshire	875.2	258	2013	73	27.57	—	—	4:30
Test Matches	†179.1 155.5	82	734	24	30.58	—	—	4:51
Other Matches in UK	509	164	1121	53	21.15	2	—	6:20
Other Matches in Australia	†196	26	608	23	26.43	4	1	6:145
Other Matches in West Indies	424.5	128	1003	34	29.50	2	—	7:50
TOTALS	†375.1 9188.4	3360	18320	991	18.48	47	10	8:26

†8-Ball overs.

CENTURIES

206*	Yorkshire v. Derbyshire at Sheffield, 1920
169	Yorkshire v. Gloucestershire at Bristol, 1914
166	Yorkshire v. Northamptonshire at Northampton, 1921
150	Yorkshire v. Northamptonshire at Harrogate, 1921
150	Yorkshire v. Middlesex at Lord's, 1926
137	Yorkshire v. Nottinghamshire at Nottingham, 1920
124	Yorkshire v. Northamptonshire at Leeds, 1922
124	Yorkshire v. Warwickshire at Dewsbury, 1925
121	Yorkshire v. Warwickshire at Birmingham, 1920
120	Yorkshire v. MCC at Lord's, 1919
117	Yorkshire v. Worcestershire at Dudley, 1922
115*	Yorkshire v. Gloucestershire at Leeds, 1919
113	Players v Gentlemen at Lord's, 1924
112	Yorkshire v. Gloucestershire at Gloucester, 1919
104	Yorkshire v. Leicestershire at Leeds, 1913
103	MCC v. Western Australia at Perth, 1924-25
100*	Yorkshire v. MCC at Scarborough, 1925

Figure 1.64. A summary of Roy Kilner's cricketing achievements.

Australia won the game by a mere eleven runs.

Kilner's personality was outgoing and popular and in his benefit year of 1925 £4,106 was raised, a good indication of his popularity. In the 1926 season he toured the West Indies and played in four tests against Australia. In 1927, after failing to take 100 wickets in a season for the first time in six years, he accepted an invitation from the Maharajah of Patiala to coach in India. He had played there in 1922-23 and 1923-24. On a previous visit he had scored 283 not out and become a cricketing legend.

On the trip home he was taken ill at Marseilles. Kilner had been engaged to give a display of cricketing skills at Gamages' store in London but was far too ill and was taken home, to Wombwell, by ambulance before being admitted to Kendray hospital where it was confirmed that he had enteric fever. He died on 5 April 1928, aged thirty-seven.

Roy Kilner's funeral was a memorable and sad occasion. It was one of the biggest funerals Wombwell had ever seen. More than 100,000 mourners were on the streets to bid farewell to one of the most respected and loved cricketers to represent the white rose (Figure 1.64).

WORSBROUGH, ST MARY'S CHURCH AND CHURCHYARD
Roger Rockley d.1533, a proud Tudor knight

A most remarkable Tudor two-tier monument can be seen in the south side of the chancel of St Mary's Church. Mainly of oak, with an effigy on each 'bunk', it commemorates a local knight, Sir Roger Rockley who died in 1533 aged about thirty-three (Figures 1.65 and 1.66). The upper effigy portrays the Knight as a handsome figure in armour, his hands in a position of prayer and his gaze heavenwards. Below is a grim cadaver, his figure as a skeleton, draped with a

shroud, a grim reminder of mortality. The whole rests on a tomb chest containing carved armourial shields. Sixteenth-century craftsmen had covered the timber effigies with strips of linen which were then painted in order to give a 'life-like' appearance but the entire composition harks back to a medieval rather than contemporary style. In his will of 1522 Rockley provided gifts to maidens and singlemen married at Worsbrough Church during the seven years after his

Figure 1.65. The Rockley Monument. *Brian Elliott*

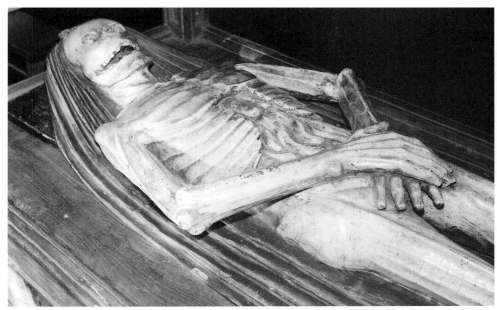

Figure 1.66. The Rockley Monument: detail of the 'grim' cadaver. *Brian Elliott*

Figure 1.67. Worsbrough Hall, home of the Edmunds family. *Brian Elliott*

Figure 1.68. Memorial tablet to Henry and Thomas Edmunds.
Brian Elliott

death. He also bequeathed provision for hospitality for travellers for fifteen years after his decease.

Henry and Thomas Edmunds d.1709, brotherly love.

Another memorial in Worsbrough Church with a story to tell concerns brothers Thomas and Henry Edmunds of Worsbrough Hall (Figure 1.67) who died on the same day, 22 March 1709. Henry, the elder brother, was the elder son and heir to Thomas Edmunds (c1556-1662) of Worsbrough who served as secretary to the illustrious Thomas Wentworth, 1st Earl of Strafford. His second wife, Elizabeth, had been married to Sir Thomas Herbert, the faithful attendant to King Charles I who was captured and imprisoned. Elizabeth brought to Worsbrough Hall some keepsakes (including several grim items) relating to the executed King Charles, in particular his footstool, a cabinet, his bloodstained cloak and his bed linen. Henry's younger brother, Thomas, married the daughter of John Wentworth of Bretton and had four sons. He had industrial interests in North Yorkshire, for in his will he refers to the lease of alum works in Cleveland. The brothers were very close, sharing the joys and disappointments of life. Their memorial tablet (Figure 1.68) is inscribed in Latin, but a translation emphasises their mutual fraternity:

> *Brothers in everything who for many years lived*
> *together on terms of the greatest friendship and*
> *brotherly love as if actuated by one spirit.*
> *Both were well and ill together and gave up*
> *their souls to God on 22 March 1709.*
> *One love, one death, one affection unite them.*
> *Who would wish a different death?*

Figure 1.69. The Field family grave. *Brian Elliott*

Figure 1.70. The ironworks at Worsbrough Bridge

John Field, c1796-1840, iron and coal pioneer

An interesting table-top monument to the Field family of Marrow House (Figure 1.69) is situated in St Mary's churchyard. John Field, initially with Messrs Cochrane and Faulds and later with Faulds and Coopers, managed ironworks at Worsbrough Bridge (Figure 1.70). But Field also had coal mining interests, leasing land from the Edmunds family in 1831 and had been manager of Edmunds Main Colliery. The distinctive monument, originally entirely enclosed by wrought iron, includes reference to Anne Field (d.1844) and Harriet Field (d.1866) and informs us that John Field Esquire was formerly of Low Moor, Bradfield 'but late of Marrow House' at Worsbrough

Figure 1.71. St Thomas' Church and churchyard. *Brian Elliott*

Figure 1.72. William Newman's grave. *Brian Elliott*

Bridge, his death 'deeply regretted by his Family and Friends'.

WORSBROUGH, ST THOMAS' CHURCH-YARD
William Newman 1789-1870, solicitor

William Newman's pink granite and mock-medieval monument contrasts with the soot-blackened upright head-stones of local mining families in St Thomas' churchyard (Figures 1.71-73). Newman was a prominent solicitor who also acted as agent to Earl Fitzwilliam. As befitting his status, he lived at Darley Cliffe Hall, a small country house of considerable charm, had the benefit of four servants and was

Death of William Newman, Esq., of Darley Hall.

We regret having to announce the death of William Newman, Esq., which took place at his residence, Darley Hall, near Worsbro', on Wednesday morning last. Mr. Newman has been so long and so intimately connected with the town and district and has been held in such deserved esteem by all whom he has had intercourse, that something more than the mere bald obituary notice is required at our hands. The deceased gentleman, who was in his 84th year, was a native of Wentworth and was nephew to the late Charles Bownes, Esq., many years agent for the Wentworth estates, first under the Marquis of Rockingham and latterly under the Earls Fitzwilliam. In this agency he was succeeded by deceased, who held the appointment until a comparatively recent period, his successor being Mr. George Rhodes, of Car House, Rotherham. The late Mr. Newman resided during the largest portion of his life in the neighbourhood of Barnsley, first at Mount Vernon, and latterly at Darley Hall, to which place he removed on the death of Mr. Bownes. He was also intimately connected with Barnsley professionally, having, as a solicitor, been many years in partnership with his brother, Edward Newman, Esq., J.P. Mr. Newman married Miss Jepson, of Hosterfield, near Doncaster, who survives him with a pretty numerous family. Alike in public and private life, Mr. Newman has been held in the highest estimation, and his acts of unostentatious benevolence were very numerous. As a tried and consistent supporter of the Liberal cause in this district; as a high-minded and upright man of business; and as a benevolent, kind-hearted christain gentleman, his name will be held in remembrance for many years to come. We understand his remains will be interred at Worsbro' Dale burial ground this day (Saturday.)

Figure 1.73. Obituary notice relating to William Newman.

Figure 1.74. Darley Cliffe Hall. *Brian Elliott*

surrounded by fine furniture, silverware, china and high quality personal effects. Newman had established one of the premier legal practices in Barnsley. He was survived by his widow, Elizabeth and five middle-aged and unmarried daughters, 'Misses Newman', aged forty-two to fifty.

II THE DONCASTER AREA

This wealthy and beautiful town
has been a place of great importance,
both in its civil and ecclesiastical character,
through the whole period of our national history.

From: South Yorkshire [vol.1] *The History and Topography of the Deanery of Doncaster, in the Diocese and County of York*, by Rev. Joseph Hunter, published in London 1828.

Figure 2.1. St George's Church, Doncaster, completed between 1854 and 1858 and one of Sir Gilbert Scott's most impressive commissions, was described as 'cathedral-like' by the eminent architectural historian Sir Nicholas Pevsner.

Figure 2.2. All Saints, Arksey, is a Norman cruciform church with a thirteenth-century crossing spire and later medieval additions. The church underwent a major restoration in 1870. *Brian Elliott*

ARKSEY, ALL SAINTS' CHURCH
Robert Portington d.1660, Civil War soldier killed by an ape bite
During the Civil War Portington was a major in Sir William Saville's regiment. He was well-known for his attachment to the Royal cause and for his courage as an officer. Afterwards he retired from the army and returned to Arksey village (Figure 2.2). However, when

Figure 2.3. *'When did you last see your father?'* was painted by W.F. Yeames (1835-1918). It depicts Cromwell's troops who have forced their way into a Royalist house trying to extract from the children the whereabouts of their father. Cromwell's men made many such visits to houses such as Robert Portington's.

Cromwell assumed the Protectorship he recalled Major Portington's allegiance to the king and despatched a troop of soldiers to Arksey in order to arrest him. The major was tipped off about the soldiers' imminent arrival, hiding in a hay-loft. Cromwell's troops (Figure 2.3) searched every part of his house and outbuildings. They saw piles of hay where he was hiding and thrust their swords into this area. A blade pierced his breast but he remained quiet and escaped detection. Portington later tried to make good his escape but Cromwell's men who were continuing to search the area, captured him and conveyed him to Hull. Unfortunately and bizarrely, he was bitten by a caged ape which he tried to pet on the ferry, later dying from the infection which developed in the wound. His monument, set inside the church, has the following inscription:

> *Draw near dear reader boldly*
> *who saw here thou art if honest and loyal to thy king*
> *if not be gone immediately*
> *less peradventure thy heel should unknowingly press*
> *These pious ashes the remains of Roger Portington*
> *which lie below, can ill bear a rebels foot*
> *unshaken by rapine by injuries and imprisonment*
> *worn out with old age and year only he fell asleep*
> *here he lies with Jane his Wife*
> *waiting for the sound of the last Trumpet*

Robert Portington interred then in the church, a general, a brave soldier and faithful to his Prince, he died the 23rd day of December in the year of our Lord 1660.

Arksey Cemetery
The Bentley Colliery Disaster Memorial, 20 November 1931

The disaster (Figure 2.4) occurred on a Friday whilst the afternoon shift was in the process of coal extraction. The explosion was reported as the worst since Cadeby in recent times. It occurred in the south-east district of the pit. The men were working in stalls 140 to 148 with an average of five men to each stall. It detonated at around 5.45p.m. and the blast travelled some 330 yards. After the alarm was raised Mine Rescue was called in from Wheatley and the neighbouring collieries of Brodsworth, Bullcroft and Edlington (Yorkshire Main). The rescue party found the district devastated and burning, which hindered their work. Mr Donald McGregor, the local mines inspector, supervised the rescue effort.

South Yorkshire Times

and Mexborough & Swinton Times.

| QUARTER. | (Established . 1877) | FRIDAY, NOVEMBER 27, 1931. | 20 PAGES—140 CO |

Calamity Comes to South Yorkshire

DISASTER AT BENTLEY

43 MEN KILLED IN PIT EXPLOSION.

WORST SINCE CADEBY.

TWICE-AFFLICTED VILLAGE

FIRE FOLLOWS FLOOD.

An appalling disaster occurred on Friday evening in the Bentley Colliery, an explosion in the south-eastern district in which over 40 men lost their lives. These men were working for the most part in the stalls numbered from 140 to 148, an average of five men in each stall.

According to an official statement the explosion occurred at 5-45 and swept the coal face for a distance of 350 yards. All the men in the direct path of the explosion were either killed outright or fatally injured.

The colliery brigade was immediately summoned and descended the pit fully equipped within a few minutes of the alarm. Later contingents were sent from the mines rescue station at Wheatley, and from the neighbouring collieries of Bullcroft, Brodsworth and Edlington.

The rescue parties found the affected district wrecked and burning and the work of rescue was slow, tedious and hazardous. There was no lack of personnel for the rescue operations, which were conducted by local mines inspector Mr. Donald MacGregor (who is also agent for the colliery), the mines manager, Mr. A. Longden, the chief engineer, Mr. J. Stafford, and others.

The whole of the miners (about 1,000) in all districts were speedily withdrawn and there was an eager response to a call for ambulance men. The first cases were taken to the old infirmary, but the accommodation there was soon exhausted and 51 beds in the new infirmary were prepared.

A second explosion occurred about 11-15 p.m. and two of the rescue party received

Thomas Hannon (15), 2a, Warmsworth Road, Doncaster;

The Bentley Colliery, which is owned by Barber, Walker and Co., Ltd., in conjunction with the Eastwood and Harworth pits, was one of the first to be sunk in the Doncaster coalfields (in 1908) and is completely modern in equipment, employing several thousand men.

ROYAL SYMPATHY.

A message of sympathy was received by the afflicted village from the King and Queen, through the Lord Lieutenant of the West Riding, Lord Harewood.

Later, the Mayor of Doncaster received notification of the desire of the King to contribute £100, and of the Queen to contribute £50, to the relief fund.

Mr. Isaac Foot, M.P., Secretary for Mines, has received from the French Minister of Public Works a message of sympathy.

Messages of sympathy were sent by Herr Husemann on behalf of German miners; M. Delattre, secretary of the International Miners' Federation; from the general secretary of the Trade Union Congress; the Northern District, National Union of Railwaymen; and every district of the Miners' Federation.

At all meetings of local authorities in South Yorkshire this week, the members have stood in silence before commencing business, to pass a vote of sympathy.

COMMONS QUESTIONS.

A GOLDTHORPE VICTIM.

IDENTIFIED BY SWEETHEART'S BROTHER.

FINE FOOTBALLER.

Clifford Wilcock, 37, Beaver Street, Goldthorpe. Wilcock, who was 25 years of age, was engaged to Miss May Thompson, a Bentley girl, and the couple were to have been married next Easter. His body was one of the first to be brought out of the pit early on Saturday morning. He was read when discovered by the rescue party, and his body was identified by his sweetheart's brother, Mr. Joseph Thompson. Since leaving the Goldthorpe Council School at the age of 14, Wilcock had worked in the Hickleton Main Colliery

Clifford Wilcock.

until a year ago, when the opportunity of a better job at Bentley offered. He was a keen footballer, and was a member of the Goldthorpe United team which in 1926-27 won many local trophies. Subsequently he played for Highgate, and at the time of his death was a member of the Bentley Colliery team. He was a fine left full-back, and had been offered trials with Grimsby and Birmingham. One of Wilcock's relatives said to a representative of the South Yorkshire Times: "Only the Sunday before it happened he was here playing with the children and promising what he would buy them for Christmas." Wilcock's mother is dead, but he is survived by his father and sister.

TOLL OF THE BRAVE.

(By ISAAC BURNS.)

The mining fraternity in general and the Bentley people in particular, seem destined to tread the path of sorrow and suffering. Twenty years ago Bentley inhabitants were plunged in grief by a colliery explosion. During the sitting of the Government Commission on Land Subsidence had given in evidence that Bentley had sunk 4ft. 6in., with costly dislocation of the sewage system. Last September Bentley was subjected to flood, the woeful consequences of which could not be conceived except by those who actually saw the destruction.

Now comes another explosion at Bentley. Death and destruction in the pit; in the

Figure 2.4. Newspaper headline relating to the Bentley Colliery disaster, *South Yorkshire Times*, 27 November 1931

About one thousand men were evacuated from the other districts in the pit. At 11.15p.m. a second explosion took place injuring two of the rescue party. By midnight twenty-nine men had been rescued and taken to a temporary hospital which had been set up nearby. Fourteen dead had been found. By Tuesday the number of bodies had risen to forty-three. Five men were unaccounted for and the decision to seal off the district was made as any further attempt to recover bodies was deemed to be too dangerous.

Barber, Walker and Company owned Bentley Colliery (Figure 2.5), as well as the Eastwood and Harworth pits. It was one of the first to be sunk in the Doncaster area, in 1908. It was regarded as thoroughly modern in its day and employed several thousand men. The King and Queen sent their tributes and messages of sympathy through the Lord Lieutenant of the West Riding, Lord Harewood, and later their Majesties contributed to the relief fund.

Memories continue to linger in local minds how news of the terrible explosion trickled into the community and how the members of Working Men's Clubs, and pubs and villagers at large rushed to aid their relatives, neighbours and friends. Tales abound of how some of the injured, in the face of their own likely deaths and racked with excruciating pain, told rescue workers to give help to others whom

Figure 2.5. Bentley Colliery was one of the largest and most modern in the Yorkshire region.

Figure 2.6. "Bentley Remembers". An annual service of remembrance continues to take place at the memorial.

they felt could be saved.

The memorial (Figures 2.6-2.7), in the form of an obelisk some ten feet six inches high, stands in the centre of the graves. It was designed by Mr Walton of the Bentley Colliery staff and its construction was supervised by Mr Stafford, the colliery engineer, and Mr Woodhall, the Bentley Council surveyor. The graves have small name-stones set at their

Figure 2.7. The memorial also commemorates the seven men killed in the Bentley Colliery disaster of 1978. *Brian Elliott*

heads. Like all pit disasters, orphans, widows and distraught parents were left to grieve, illustrating once again the terrible price of coal.

The casualty list was as follows:

Dead

Henry Womack	(44)	9 Fisher Street, Bentley
George Singleton	(31)	41 Raymond Road, Doncaster
Joseph William Grain	(35)	24 Hawthorne Grove, Bentley
Clifford Willcocks	(25)	31 Beevor Street, Goldthorpe
Alfred Hibbert	(?)	3 New Street, Bentley
Richard Derrick	(53)	35 Frank Road, Bentley
Joseph Pritchit	(40)	17 Balfour Road, Bentley
James Hargreaves	(?)	10 Balfour Road, Bentley
William Farnsworth	(34)	17 Cromwell Road, Doncaster
Samuel William Templeman	(46)	13 Cross Street, Bentley
Harry Beastle	(?)	97 The Avenue, Bentley
Thomas Green	(42)	33 Arthur Street, Bentley
L Guy	(35)	90 High Street, Bentley
William Agnu	(34)	5 Halmshaw Terrace, Bentley
Clifford Hayes	(25)	15 Cross Street, Bentley
John Callaghan	(37)	32 Milton Street, Doncaster
William Ward	(41)	60 Hawthorne Grove, Bentley
James Allsop	(26)	36 The Avenue, Bentley
Harold Lawton	(37)	34 Winnipeg Road, Bentley
Horace Windle	(36)	72 Acacia Avenue, Skellow
Albert Barcock	(17)	77 Dam Road, Bentley
John Peck	(34)	Hallvilla Road, Tollbar, Bentley
William Middleton	(31)	4 Fisher Street, Bentley
Lawrence Sleath	(25)	20 Hawthorne Grove, Bentley
George Robert Bentley	(46)	56 Arthur Street, Bentley
Herbert Cheetham	(30)	31 Victoria Road, Bentley
John Llewelli	(47)	27 Cromwell Road, Doncaster
Thomas Hopkinson	(33)	35 Daw Lane, Bentley
Daniel Maloney	(35)	14 Grove Street, Adwick-le-Street
Leonard Jones	(25)	111 Marshgate, Doncaster
Albert Hookaby	(29)	Arksey Lane, New Village, Bentley
Stanley Boxton	(28)	Ivy Dene, Tilts Lane, Tollbar, Bentley
James Leyland	(44)	34 Hallgate, Doncaster
Ernest Cawood	(50)	145 Askern Road, Bentley
John Brett	(34)	25 Asquith Road, Bentley
Charles Atkinson	(36)	28 Asquith Road, Bentley
Thomas Brown	(31)	1 Wainwright Road, Doncaster

Missing

Sam Mason	(?)	39 The Avenue, Bentley
J H Smith	(24)	9 Wheatley Park Road, Bentley
J W Rowe	(44)	15 Coney Road, Tollbar, Bentley
William Brocklehurst	(45)	13 Coney Road, Tollbar, Bentley
T Dove	(?)	67 Asquith Road, Bentley

BARNBY DUN, CHURCH OF ST PETER AND PAUL
Francis Gregory Esquire d.1671, Saxon descendant

The Saxons (Figure 2.8) were a Germanic people who began raiding the coast of Britain in the 5th century AD. By the 8th century Saxon settlements with typical place-name elements such as '-ley' and '-ton' were widespread. With the new generations of British-born Saxons evolved a new language and people: the Anglo-Saxon. After the Norman invasion of 1066 the Anglo-Saxons were subjected and forced to accept a new ruler. For centuries, however, the Saxon tradition was kept alive by certain families who continued to boast their origins; families such as the Gregories of Barnby Dun.

An inscription inside the church reads:

Figure 2.8. Arms and costume of a Saxon military chief.

To the pious memory of
Francis Gregory esq.,
who departed this life August 11th 1671,
who was the Son of William,
the Son of Roger Gregorie esq.,
who came in with the Saxons and
situated themselves at Stick Hill, in
Warwickshire, from thence they moved to
Stockwith in the County of Lincoln,
from thence
the eldest brother William came to
Barnby Dun in the County of York.

BRODSWORTH, ST MICHAEL'S CHURCH
Herbert Adams c.1881-1901, Boer War casualty

The discovery of major goldfields in the Transvaal in the 1890s sparked clashes between the Dutch and British settlers. The war was

Figure 2.9. The Yorkshire Light Infantry was part of the attack on Kimberley and pursued General Cronje following his retreat and captured him near Paardeburg. When he surrendered he still had 4,000 troops with him.

partly precipitated by the arrival of the Germans in South Africa and their threat to the colony, trade and routes to India. The Dutch welcomed the intrusion of the Germans and Paul Krüger, the elected leader of the Transvaal, offered the hand of friendship to them. It appeared to the government that, unless firm action was taken, the Germans and Dutch would restrict any chance of Britain's northward expansion and isolate her in the Cape province. The Boers outnumbered the 25,000 British troops stationed in the country by two to one. The British Government sent reinforcements from India and the Mediterranean to South Africa to assemble a formidable fighting force. A fresh corps of 48,000 men landed and was swelled by further troops from England. Herbert Adams of Pickburn was one of these soldiers. The Yorkshire Light Infantry arrived in the colony in 1899 (Figure 2.9). By the end of February 1900 the Infantry had been involved in various actions, including the relief of Kimberley and the capture of General Cronje with 48,000 men. Soon after Blöemfontein, the capital of the Orange Free State, and Ladysmith were also taken. Natal was abandoned by the Boers. During this period fever laid low many of the British troops. Sadly, while his regiment was at Charlestown, Herbert succumbed.

On 31 May 1902 the Treaty of Vereeniging was signed bringing the war to an end. Under the terms of the treaty the British Government

Figure 2.10. St Michael's Church at Brodsworth. *Brian Elliott*

agreed to pay £3 million to repair damaged farms and make loans interest-free for two years to re-settle farmers. More importantly, a British-run government was sworn in to administer the Transvaal and the Orange Free State. As far as the British Government was concerned the crisis was over.

Herbert's memorial tablet is fixed to the wall by the main entrance to St Michael's Church, Brodsworth (Figure 2.10).

The inscription reads as follows:

> *In loving memory of Herbert, the beloved son of*
> *George and Frances Adams (Pickburn). A Private*
> *in the King's Own Yorkshire Light Infantry who*
> *died of Enteric Fever May 12th 1901 at Charlestown,*
> *South Africa aged 20 years.*

CADEBY, THE CHURCH OF ST JOHN
George Harry Wyatt VC c1881-1964, First World War hero

Lance Corporal G.H. Wyatt, 5854 (Figure 2.11), was serving in the 3rd Battalion, Coldsteam Guards in the very early days of the First World War. On 25 August 1914, at Landreces, he twice dashed out of the line under heavy fire to extinguish burning straw which threatened to make his unit's position untenable. At Villers Cotterets a few days later he was wounded in the head but continued fighting

until the flow of blood blinded him. After his wound was dressed he returned to the firing line and resumed fighting.

For these acts of exceptional courage George Wyatt was awarded Britain's highest recognition for bravery in the field, the Victoria Cross. He received a civic welcome and a dinner in his honour, at the Mansion House, on his return from leave in April 1915.

George Wyatt survived the war. On his discharge from the army he joined the police (Figure 2.12) and attained the rank of Sergeant. He was a well-known public figure.

He died on 22 January 1964, aged seventy-seven. On his gravestone, on the

Figure 2.11. Lt Cpl G.H. Wyatt, 3rd Coldstream Guards: VC for heroism at Landrecies.

Figure 2.12. Harry Wyatt (left) receives the congratulations of a police officer in Doncaster (St Sepulchre Gate).

Figure 2.13. The small but attractive church of St John at Cadeby was completed in about 1856 by Sir Gilbert Scott who was also working on a much larger project: St George's Church in Doncaster. *Brian Elliott*

Figure 2.14. The grave of George Harry Wyatt, VC. *Brian Elliott*

near left side of Cadeby churchyard (Figures 2.13-2.14) is the badge of the Coldstream Guards and a masonic symbol.

CONISBROUGH CEMETERY
Carleton Henry Allport c1854-1916, author and antiquarian

C.H. Allport carried out extensive research into the history of Conisbrough, no doubt influenced by its dramatic castle and the ancient church of St Peter. In 1913 he published the *History of Conisborough* (Figure 2.15) It serves as an invaluable reference book for Conisbrough and the surrounding area. Allport died on 29 May 1916, aged sixty-two.

Allport's memorial can be found by taking the right-hand path off the main drive beyond the house. It is on the left and surmounted by a fine stone anchor.

By profession Allport worked as an insurance broker and, as can be seen in Figure 2.16, displayed a somewhat curious notice in his Church Street shop.

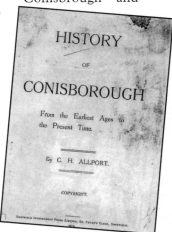

Figure 2.15. Title page from Allports *History*.

Figure 2.16. Notice placed in the window of C.H. Allport's shop

Dearne, Mexborough and Rawmarsh Edition

Friday, July 22nd, 1988   **Price 20p**

Conisbrough was celebrating a unique double heart-transplant success story this week when tragedy struck. As the news broke of another operation, the town was shocked to learn of the death of Pauline Smith, who received a new heart four years ago.

THE JOY...

Heart-transplant gran Yvonne Walton was up and about only a week after undergoing her lifesaving operation.

By Debbie Smith

At 55 Yvonne, of Conan Road, Conisbrough, is believed to be one of the oldest people in the country to have a heart transplant, and surgeons are said to be "very pleased" with her progress.

Last Wednesday Mrs. Walton was called to the Freeman Hospital, Newcastle and in the early hours of Thursday morning underwent the major operation which her family hope will give her a new lease of life.

Yvonne suffered the first of three heart attacks about six years ago, and seemed to recover, according to her youngest daughter, Lesley.

However, she had another two attacks which damaged her heart and left her very ill.

Lesley said, "She has always been very active and worked until about two years ago at Conisbrough Northcliffe School as a dinner lady, and still enjoyed gardening.

"She wants her independence, and to get back to a normal life".

Yvonne's husband, former Conisbrough Councillor, Dick Walton, has been at his wife's side since last week and is staying at a flat in the hospital.

She had been going to the Northern General Hospital, Sheffield for treatment but in February Yvonne travelled to Newcastle for

● Yvonne Walton

tests, and was very calm when she received the news summoning her last week.

At the weekend her two daughters, Lesley (21) and Carol (37) went to Newcastle to see her, "We were amazed to see her walking around and looking healthier than she has for years".

A spokeswoman for the hospital said, "The operation went very well and we are very pleased with her progress but it will be quite a while before she will be allowed home".

...THE SORROW

Brave Conisbrough landlady Pauline Smith who in September 1983 became the fifth woman to receive a heart transplant at Papworth Hospital, died on Wednesday morning aged 47.

Pauline, mother of two, had a set-back earlier this year when kidney failure resulted in her needing hospital dialysis treatment three times a week. Her husband David said the family were devastated.

By Anne Story

"Pauline was rushed into the Hallamshire Hospital on Tuesday night and she died at 7.30a.m. this morning", he said on Wednesday. "She had not been too well this year

and had regularly been visiting hospital", he added.

Sharing his grief were son Mark (21) and daughter Carron (17).

The family had shown their gratitude to the Cambridge Hospital ever since the heart transplant operation on September 22nd, 1983. They encouraged family, friends and customers to fund-raise over the past five years.

The couple took over the Hilltop pub in January 1986, when Pauline welcomed the new life, wanting to put behind them the trauma of years of illness leading to the transplant operation and the gradual recovery after the operation.

Pauline felt she was ready for a new challenge and at that time said she felt 90 per cent fit. She believed every day was a bonus.

Pauline was eternally grateful for the new life given to her by the team at Pap-

● Pauline and David

worth and she met another local transplant patient Davina Thompson shortly after her heart-transplant in December 1986, offering the Thompson family hope and advice for the future.

Pauline and her family, who formerly lived in Old Road, Conisbrough, enjoyed the new life created when they took over the pub. David had formerly worked on the oil rigs, but gave up the job to be at home with Pauline after the transplant.

Pauline, who was born in Conisbrough, had worked at the South

Yorkshire Times Printing Company in her young day and was also a barmaid at Balby. She and David would have celebrated their Silver wedding anniversary next year.

She was desperately ill for 18 months before the operation, her life being saved in 1982 when her heart stopped whilst on a routine visit to Doncaster Royal Infirmary.

She was a quiet person, who rarely talked about her experiences and was grateful for every day she had been given by the team at Papworth.

Figure 2.17. News headline from the *South Yorkshire Times* relating to the death of Pauline Smith.

Pauline Smith (nee Clewer) c1942-1988, pioneering heart transplant patient

Pauline Smith was the fifth woman in the United Kingdom to undergo a heart transplant operation, in September 1983. She lived at *Hill Top Hotel* where she was landlady, and died on 20 July 1988, aged forty-six. After the pioneering operation Pauline understandably received a lot of publicity (Figure 2.17) but rose to the occasion in order to encourage fellow sufferers and advance medical research. The operation proved successful in that it prolonged her life five years beyond her doctor's prognosis. She helped the medical profession in the new service of transplant surgery.

Her grave is located just over the brow of the hill on the left of the cemetery chapel.

DENABY MAIN CEMETERY
John Grainger, Bag Muck Strike Test Case, 1902-3

Denaby Main Colliery (Figures 2.18-2.19) started production in 1868. Cadeby, one mile distant, was sunk in 1893. By the early 1900s both collieries were owned by the Denaby and Cadeby Colliery Company which was a successful industrial undertaking employing more than 4,000 men and producing more than one million tons of coal a year. The company also had its own railway and shipping interests.

John Grainger, buried in Denaby Main Cemetery, was named in

Figure 2.18. Denaby Main Colliery

Figure 2.19. 1950s view from the old passenger bridge showing Denaby Main Colliery (on left), with traffic queuing to let a steam train through.

an initial legal test case in a landmark industrial dispute during which many families were forcibly evicted from company houses and subjected to terrible hardship.

Trouble started in 1902 when the traditional thin band of earth (known as 'muck') which separated the Barnsley seam, called the 'day bed', from its low portion, known as the 'bags'. This layer of earth became known as the 'bag muck'. Historically the bag muck had been four inches to ten inches thick and proved no problem to the miners. In 1901, however, the thickness of the layer started to increase and widened to thirty-six inches. This was a severe blow to the men who were paid on the basis of the actual coal produced. This obstacle impeded coal extraction and, consequently, wages. The bag muck affected about a hundred miners working in the Melton drift who were a small percentage of the total workforce.

A meeting was called at which the feeling was expressed that the miners affected should receive extra payments due to the time they had needed to spend removing the muck band. The company would not hear of it. In 1890 a contract price had been negotiated and the colliery company was sticking to that agreement.

In September 1901 a ballot of the miners failed to get the required two-thirds majority for strike action.

As the months dragged by the problem continued to aggravate. In February 1902 the Yorkshire Miners' Association took the case to Doncaster County Court as the company had deducted wages from certain miners who had refused to remove the bag muck and thus created an obstruction. The company's view was that the money deducted would be used to pay other men who would do the work of clearing the muck away. John Grainger was selected as a test case. He had 17s 9d (89p) stopped from his wages. Judge Masterman ruled for the colliery company.

At the *Reresby Arms* public house (now the *Milestone*), situated across the road from Denaby Main Colliery a mass meeting of over 3,000 men took place and it was decided that, after the failure of John Grainger's case, strike action must take place. The pits were closed in celebration of the coronation of King Edward VII in June 1902 and did not re-open after the holiday.

Figure 2.20. Evictions at Denaby. From *Mexborough and Swinton Times*, 9 January 1903.

On 2 July 1902, a meeting was arranged with Mr Chambers, the manager, but no satisfactory outcome was reached. As the company had not been given proper notice the strike was unofficial and the Yorkshire Miners' Association could not issue strike pay. This resulted in many cases of hardship in the Denaby area. It was decided to return to work and serve the company the required two weeks' notice of the strike. But the company refused to allow the men back and they were locked out unless they agreed to sign a new contract.

The strike dragged on until 19 August 1902 when the company closed down both pits. As property owners, the company sent notices to quit to 750 strikers who had fallen behind with their rents. On 6 January the following year, bailiffs and two hundred police began evicting some 2,000 people from their homes in Firbeck Street, Cliff View and Edlington Street (Figure 2.20). The families had to take shelter where they could, in tents, chapels and barns, and the spare rooms of supporters. The Yorkshire Miners' Association was taken to court and a claim for £150,000 damages was lost at first.

By 22 March, with family circumstances becoming dire and support evaporating, men started drifting back to work. Even by the end of April a thousand men still held out and by July five hundred remained defiant. The colliery company continued with their appeal against the original judgment and took it to the House of Lords where they lost, the Lords finding for the Yorkshire miners. Although John Grainger was the test case for the Bag Muck Strike, he was of course only one of the many who suffered great hardship.

DONCASTER CEMETERY
William Hardy c1845-1887, rail crash victim

The St Leger Week of 1887 was marred by a great tragedy. An awful collision occurred when the Liverpool to Hull express ran into the back of a Midland rail excursion which was standing at the platform at Hexthorpe. The Midland train had left Sheffield and picked up more racegoers at Rotherham and was waiting in the station while tickets were being checked. The Liverpool to Hull express had left Manchester at 10.00a.m. and made its way towards Doncaster, unaware of what lay ahead.

Two of the Midland carriages were crushed to pieces and broken wood and cushions were strewn all over the track. Fifteen occupants of the two coaches were killed outright and nine others died soon afterwards. A large group of medical men was called to the scene and there was a frantic atmosphere as every passenger was checked. The

APPALLING RAILWAY CALAMITY AT DONCASTER.

24 KILLED AND MANY INJURED.

The St. Leger week has been marred by a terrible calamity, and the Cup Day of 1887 will long be remembered on account of the awful collision on the railway which convulsed not only Doncaster, but the whole district for miles around from an early hour yesterday afternoon. It seems that a Midland train from Sheffield had drawn up at Hexthorpe, and tickets were being collected. Work was nearly done when an M. S. and L. express, leaving Manchester at 10 o'clock, dashed into the rear of the stationary train. Two long bogie Midland carriages were instantly dashed to pieces, and crushed to a mere shell, the broken wood, and even cushions, littering the line. Fifteen of the occupants were killed outright, and others died shortly afterwards. Some victims were literally disembowelled, and mangled beyond recognition. The dead were laid out in an adjoining field, and promptly removed to Doncaster. A large staff of medical men were on the spot relieving the sufferers, who were taken to Doncaster Infirmary. The engine-driver, a Manchester man, named Taylor, was badly hurt. The accident is reported to have been caused by a mistake at the signals, which were said to be against the driver.

The stationary Midland train suffered the most injury. None of the occupants of the Manchester Sheffield and Lincolnshire train suffered injury, but those in the Midland were not nearly so fortunate. Mr T. Trimnell, solicitor, London, son of Mr Trimnell, late organist at the Sheffield Parish Church, had both legs broken. Drs. Martin and Thorpe were in one of the trains, and themselves uninjured rendered valuable surgical help to the many injured around. The occupants of both trains were far too shocked after the sights of the dead and dying they had witnessed, to proceed on their day of pleasure, and by far the greater majority returned home by the first available train. Breakdown gangs were speedily summoned by telegraph, and in the meantime traffic was worked on a single line. Both the trains were occupied by excursionists. The collision occurred almost underneath Hexthorpe Bridge, and closely adjacent to the village of that name. The pressure on the traffic at this point is tremendous during the Doncaster week, and it requires all the care of the officials to preserve the order of safety. Hexthorpe is not a passenger station, but a coal station, and is only used by the passenger officials for the purpose of collecting tickets of passengers.

It appears that a heavily laden train left Sheffield yesterday morning a little after eleven o'clock, and proceeded in safety as far as Hexthorpe. In the rear of it was a heavily laden train from Liverpool. The latter, in charge of an old and experienced driver, left Liverpool yesterday morning, at 8-40. The driver of the Liverpool train was injured, but he did his utmost in the work of recovering the dead and injured. Just before the Sheffield train left the ticket platform the engine of the Liverpool train dashed into the hindmost vehicle—the guard's van of the Sheffield train. The crash was a terrible one, and in a moment there was a pile up, mass of debris, from which groans and shrieks arose, terrible, terrible. ...

The ... Sanderson, ... Cross lane, Crookes, Sheffield.

Charles Hall, Matilda street, Sheffield.

— Connolly, Wombwell.

Anthony Fitzpatrick, Eastwood, Notts.

Arthur Foster, Brinkley, Sheffield.

Eddy Thompson, Charge lane, Highfield, Sheffield.

John Goldsmith, Royal Oak Inn, Sheffield, leg smashed.

Fred Wm. Roberson, Thomas street, Sheffield.

— Hawksworth, Leadmill road, Sheffield.

Alfred Fordyke, 31, St. Mary's road, Sheffield.

H. Jarvis, 94, Artisan view, Heeley.

T. Vernon, Union street, Sheffield, fractured leg.

Daniel Hoppe, Leadmill road, Sheffield.

Wm. Stokes, Ann Stokes, and Mary Ann Stokes, 121, Pond street, Sheffield.

Annie Burley, 277, Shoreham street, Sheffield, (13 years of age), and

Mary Burley (mother to Annie).

John Losek, Jubilee Villa, Albert road, Handsworth, near Birmingham.

Jarvis Key, Hanover street, Sheffield.

J. Connolly, Brittania Inn, Sheffield.

Henry Bocking, Red House, Fargate, Sheffield, leg hurt.

Sam Lovell, Crosspool, Sheffield.

It is understood that there are 84 injured people in the Infirmary, two dead, and six injured at Balby, and a similar number accommodated in houses around the Infirmary.

Another correspondent says:—Among the killed is Frederick Bee, aged 12, Fieldhead road, Sheffield. Among the injured is—

Mr Trimnell, son of the late Sheffield Parish Church organist, fractured leg.

24 KILLED.

As near as could be ascertained last evening there were 23 deaths.

Figure 2.21. Extract from the *Rotherham Advertiser*, Saturday 17 September 1887

dead were laid out in a field adjoining the station. The accident was caused by the Liverpool train driver, Mr Taylor, who was also badly hurt, being given the wrong signal. This section of the line was extremely busy and signal staff were stretched to control it in St Leger week. The Hexthorpe station was normally a coal station and only open for passengers in St Leger Week for the purpose of checking tickets. The passengers of the Liverpool train suffered no major injuries. Rescue teams were summoned by telegraph and an army of people appeared to clear the lines of the carnage (Figure 2.21).

William Hardy's grave can be seen after entering the main cemetery gates, turning left at the fifth tree and proceeding ten paces. His father, Joseph, had died in 1885, aged sixty-nine.

DONCASTER, ST GEORGE'S CHURCH

Surely one of the most splendid of Victorian churches, St George's is a magnificent replacement by G.B. Scott of the medieval town church of Doncaster (Figures 2.22-2.23). The churchyard contains numerous eighteenth-century gravestones, with some earlier examples extant within its 'cathedral' proportions (Figure 2.24). Any antiquarian visiting the old church during the early decades of the nineteenth century would have been impressed by the number and variety of memorials of local worthies including successful tradesmen and military men. But perhaps the most distinguished

Figure 2.22. The impressive tower of old St George's can be seen on this print of 1806.

Figure 2.23. The ruins of St George's Church, gutted by fire, 23 February 1853.

Figure 2.24. The lofty interior of the new Church of St George.

related to the church organist, a musician of more than local talent who also published the first history of the town.

Edward Miller 1735-1807, musician, composer and historian

Miller (Figure 2.25) was brought up in Norwich, the son of a paviour (and freeman of the city). Undoubtedly talented and interested in music he appears to have come under the tuition of the celebrated Dr Burney, probably in Kings Lynn as well as London. Miller's first published work, *A Collection of New English Songs and a Cantata* probably just pre-dates his appointment as organist in Doncaster, in 1756. In 1763 Miller married Miss Elizabeth Lee, daughter of Thomas Lee, a barber and peruke maker. His knowledge of the theory of music was extensive and he completed many works, including *The Institutes of Music* (1783), *Elements of Thorough Bass and Composition* (1787), *Letters on behalf of Professors of Music* (1784) and *The Psalms of David* (1790). He also composed *The Tears of Yorkshire* ... for the Marquis of Rockingham (1782), which was played at its dedicatee's funeral in York Minster.

In 1804 Miller published *The History and Antiquities of Doncaster and its Vicinity* (Figure 2.26). In preparation for this monumental task he travelled extensively in the Doncaster area, as far east as Thorne and westwards towards Wombwell. Places near Pontefract, to the north of Doncaster, and southern villages not far from Nottingham were also visited. He recorded the history of each place from conversations with residents, church records, records from landowning families and from personal observations.

Figure 2.25. Portrait of E d w a r d Miller.

The Marquis of Rockingham lobbied for him to be appointed to the vacancy as Master of His Majesty's Bands of Musicians, following the death of Dr William Boyce. The Lord Chamberlain would have supported the application. The King, however, preferred the celebrated blind organist John Stanley. Dr Miller also befriended the renowned astronomer William Herschel, helping to bring about the latter's acceptance as a scientist in society.

The inscription on Miller's marble family memorial in old St George's reads as follows:

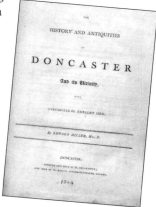

In Memory of Elizabeth, wife of Edward Miller Dr in Music. She was born August 8th, 1745: she died August 14th, 1773. Also of her three daughters Elizabeth, Mary, and Lois. And of her third son Thomas, a midshipman, who was shipwrecked in the "Haleswell" on the rocks of Purbeck. These children all died in the bloom of youth Also EDWARD MILLER, Mus. D., who died Sept. 13th, 1807, aged 72 years; nearly 52 years Organist of this Church;

Figure 2.26. Title page from Miller's 'History'.

author of "Improvement of Psalmody"
"History of Doncaster" etc etc.
After having served the world
for many years,
at last he strove to serve his God;
and there is hope that, by sincere
repentance and a lively faith in the crucified
Redeemer, he died in peace

Figure 2.27. George IV, from a painting by Sir Thomas Lawrence.

Jonathan Boardman c1703–1776, 'royal' cap maker

Boardman was well-known in the Doncaster area as 'Jonathan Caps'. His skills gained him a wide patronage but an obsession with 'exclusiveness' meant that he never took on an apprentice in order to pass on the 'mystery' of the trade. One exception, however, was Richard Backus who not only continued the business of protecting the heads of society huntsmen but also maintained the high standards set by Boardman. It was said that the Prince of Wales (later George IV) and the Duke of York rarely passed through Doncaster without insisting on placing an order (Figure 2.27). Boardmen was successful in his trade as shown by his will, proved at York on 5 October 1776. He died a bachelor and left to his cousin, the Lord Bishop of St Asaph (Dr Joseph Shipley), a diamond ring valued at twenty guineas alone which, at the time, was a small fortune, along with lands and the residue of his estate.

John Smith d.1808, whose death was a warning to bell-ringers

The inscription on the Smith family memorial testifies to a rather unfortunate accident in the bell-chamber of old St George's and a drowning:

Here lyes two sons of Robert Smith
Cord Wainer (shoemaker) *and Leader*
of the Ringers, one of whom, John,
whilst ringing, was accidentally carried
up by a rope to the floor of the bell chamber
and received injuries which caused his death
in 1808 and also, the burial of his brother
on 17th November 1812.

These two youths were, by misfortune,
surrounded. One died of his wounds
and t'other drowned

Major Edward Topham c1751-1820, soldier, writer and country gentleman

Buried in the chancel, Edward Topham was the son of Dr Francis Topham who was master of facilities and a judge at the court in York. He attended Cambridge and then commanded a commission in the 2nd Troop of the Horse Guards, rising to the rank of major. Topham received the King's Commendation for the high standard of discipline that he instilled into the soldiers in his command and for his military reforms. In the press he was caricatured as 'The Tip Top Adjutant'.

Topham possessed considerable literary talent and wrote the biography of John Elwas, a notorious miser and also *Letter from Edinburgh*, as well as several farces and a further work called *The World*. His memorial is as follows:

Sacred to the memory of Edward
Topham Esq.,
who first at Eaton and then at Trinity
College,
Cambridge, was distinguished for
scholarship.
Having subsequently for several years
engaged
through, without injury in the
excitement of public
life he retired at last to his Country
House and
there under the weight of years died
April 27th
1820, aged 69.

Topham had retired to Wold Cottage, Thwing, near Bridlington, and became a shrewd breeder of greyhounds. He had particular success with one dog called *Snowball* which became a champion distance runner. Topham also developed an interest in astronomy and wrote an account of meteorites.

Figure 2.28. Christ Church, Doncaster, from a postcard sent in 1907.

Doncaster Christ Church

John Jarratt c1744-1828, founder-benefactor of Doncaster's 'second church'

John Jarratt grew up in Doncaster but spent the greater part of his life in Bradford where he started out in the 'stuff trade', later moving to the iron works at Lowmoor where he amassed a considerable fortune.

On his retirement, Jarratt returned to Doncaster, purchasing estates at Bessecar, Balby and Hexthorpe. In 1821 he invested 2,000 guineas with the corporation for which they were to pay a bond income of 100 guineas a year. When aged eighty-three, in 1827, he proposed a design for a new church for the town of Doncaster at a time when St George's could not accommodate the growing population of the town. Drawings were put in the hands of Edmund Dennison, John Branson and Robert Baxter, along with access to 13,000 guineas. Jarratt wanted to spend 10,000 guineas on the building and 3,000 guineas on the fabric and endowment. The corporation granted two acres of land at the entrance of Thorne Road, which was a remnant quarry known as the Sandpits. The church (Figure 2.28) was built of Roche Abbey stone and consecrated on 26 June 1829, shortly after Jarratt's death.

Colonel George Holmes CB 1771-1833, veteran officer of the Napoleonic Wars

For thirty-eight years Holmes was an officer in the 3rd Dragoon Guards and for twenty of those years was Regimental Commander

and served with distinction in the Peninsular War (Figure 2.29).

Colonel Holmes was the son of Solomon Holmes, alderman of Doncaster. He was born on 12 August 1771 and at the age of twenty-four was the Cornet in the 3rd Dragoon Guards. A year later he had risen to

Figure 2.29.
Portrait of a Lieutenant Colonel (and ex-Cornet), and a contemporary of Holmes, in the uniform of the Royal Horse Guards, wearing the Waterloo medal.

Lieutenant and in 1803 was promoted to Captain. In 1809 he was appointed Major and became a Lieutenant Colonel in 1811, becoming Colonel of the regiment in 1825.

He was active at Talavera as Major of Brigade to Sir Henry Feign and also at Busaco, Los Santos, Vsagre, Maguilia, Albuera Cuidad Rodrigo, Vittoria and Toulouse. Napoleon was trying to extend his domination of Europe by invading Portugal, sending an army headed by General Junet. Portugal appealed to Britain to intervene and troops were subsequently despatched. Colonel Holmes was present at all major battles and had the satisfaction of seeing the French defeated and Portugal relieved.

Holmes became a magistrate, noted for his kindness and married Elizabeth Jemima, the daughter of Sir Egerton Bridges of Denton Court, Kent. The Colonel became Mayor of Doncaster in 1831.

EDLINGTON CEMETERY
Arthur Wharton 1865-1930, world record sprinter and first black professional footballer

In recent years, after several decades of obscurity, Arthur Wharton (Figure 2.30) has become something of a symbol for black athletes, especially footballers. The research of Phil Vasili has been instrumental in providing present and future generations with vital information and recognition about this otherwise forgotten local sportsman. Vasili's book, *The First Black Footballer* was published in 1998 (by Frank Cass, ISBN 071464903-1). At least one national radio programme has been broadcast in celebration of Wharton's achievements and a screenplay written for a TV film.

Wharton was born in James Town, Ghana (then known as the Gold Coast) in 1865, the son of a wealthy Methodist missionary. But as a young man he attended Cleveland College in County Durham. His first known sporting appearance was playing in goal for Darlington in 1884, soon attracting attention not only because of his appearance but also for his unorthodox play. Apparently, Wharton would squat in a

Figure 2.30. Arthur Wharton, sprinter and footballer, poses in a photographer's studio in the 1890s. Note bowler hat, cane and cigar.

Figure 2.31. 'The Invincibles': Preston North End, 1897. Wharton is fourth from the left.

corner of the goal and then explode into action at the very last second whenever his skills were required. It must have caused great humour and entertainment to spectators and no doubt annoyance to attacking players. One contemporary report of a fixture between Rotherham and Sheffield Wednesday, referred to Wharton catching the ball between his legs whilst hanging with both hands from the crossbar, much to the consternation of onrushing forwards who finished in the back of the 'net'! and to the great delight of the crowd. After twenty appearances with Darlington and the tag of 'best goalkeeper in the north' Wharton moved to Preston North End, but only played FA Cup games for the famous 'invincibles' (Figure 2.31), in an arrangement where he (still an amateur, at least officially) was allowed to play other fixtures for his home team. In 1886-87 Preston reached the Cup semi-final, no doubt helped by Wharton keeping a 'clean sheet' in the first four rounds of the competition. However, during the next season he played for seven different teams, a practice that hardly endeared him to Preston who dropped him from a team that created a record that still stands - a 26-0 Cup victory over Hyde.

Wharton's sporting achievements extended to athletics. He became the AAA one hundred yard sprint champion in successive years (1886-87), in effect 'the fastest man on earth' (Figure 2.32) and the first 'black' man to win an AAA championship (Figure 2.33).

Although tempted to return to Africa, Wharton married and settled in

Figure 2.32. Wharton clocking a British (in effect world) record of 'evens', 10.00 seconds in the 100 yards at Stamford Bridge, 3 July 1886.

South Yorkshire where football dominated his time. In 1889 he signed for Rotherham Town of the Midland League – initially as a centre-forward! But he soon returned to his normal position in goal, Rotherham winning two championships and considering applying for the Football League.

Despite his undoubted ability Wharton was overlooked by the international selectors, his ethnic origins certainly going against him. However, his unusual actions during some games may also have done him harm. He would, for example, have no hesitation in joining the outfield players, sometimes with dire consequences. He was also apparently guilty of occasional tantrums and

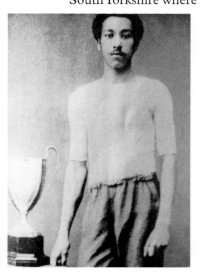

Figure 2.33. Wharton with the sprint trophy (Prince Hassan Cup) that he won for the 100 yards at Stamford Bridge on 3 July 1886. He retained the title a year later in a time of 10.1 seconds.

Figure 2.34. Wharton as a Rotherham player, c1894.

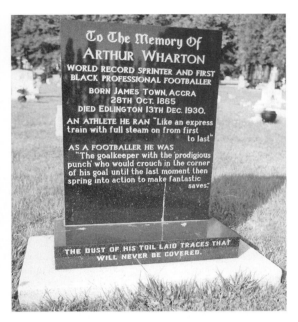

Figure 2.35. Wharton's grave, Edlington cemetery, 1999. A ceremony to unveil a new headstone on an hitherto unmarked plot took place in 1997, sixty-seven years after his death. *Brian Elliott*

frequent pay demands. It was following a pay dispute that he left Rotherham to join rivals Sheffield United, also taking over a Sheffield pub as part of the deal. His appearances for United were, however, very limited due to the formidable presence of William 'Fatty' Foulkes and he soon returned to Rotherham (Figure 2.34).

His final years in professional sport were as a football mercenary, playing for Stalybridge Rovers (as player-trainer) in 1896-97 and then Aston North End in the Lancashire League. His last known game was for Stockport County in 1902 when he was thirty-seven years old.

Arthur Wharton died in 1930 and was buried, without a headstone in Edlington cemetery, virtually a forgotten figure (Figure 2.35). In all respects he was a pioneer in a very racist society but now he has been given the respect and admiration that he thoroughly deserves as Britain's first black soccer star.

OLD EDLINGTON
The Viscount's greyhound

In 1714 Viscount Robert Molesworth had the remains of his favourite greyhound sent from London to Old Edlington where it was treated to a proper burial including a small square altar monument (Figure 2.36). The translated (from Latin) inscription read:

> *Stay Traveller*
> *No wonder that a lamented dog*
> *is thus interred with funeral honour*
> *but ah! what a dog. His beautiful form and snow white*
> *colour pleasing manners and sporting playfulness,*

affection, obedience and fidelity made
him the delight of his master
to whose side he closely adhered
with his eager companions of the chase
delighted in attending him. Whenever the mind of his Lord
was depressed, he would assume fresh spirit and animation.
A master not ungrateful for his merits, has here, in tears,
deposited his remains in this marble urn MFX 1714

The Molesworths who had a London home, had purchased the Edlington estate in 1708. The story goes that when he was going to the privy one night his faithful greyhound dragged at the flap of his coat and would not let him proceed. Robert tried again with the same response from the dog. Puzzled, he sent a servant to investigate. His man was then shot by an intruder, apparently concealed in the lavatory.

Figure 2.36. Early drawing of the marble monument dedicated to the greyhound and erected in Edlington Wood.

Figure 2.37. The *White Greyhound* Public House

The *White Greyhound* public house (Figure 2.37), on the road between Old Edlington and New Edlington, serves as a conspicuous reminder of the Molesworth story.

HARWORTH CHURCHYARD (NOTTS)
Tommy Simpson 1937-1967, world champion cyclist

Tommy Simpson (Figure 2.38) was born in Durham in 1937, the son of a miner. Following a pit accident his father moved to Harworth in search of employment. Young Tom joined the Harworth Cycling Club and excelled at the sport, winning the club twenty-five mile time trial by his sixteenth birthday.

Looking for stiffer competition he transferred to the Scala Wheelers at Rotherham where he took part in a variety of races. He competed in an international race in Russia against a Russian and Italian squad and did so well that he was selected for the British Olympic team to compete in Australia. At Melbourne he won the silver medal in the road team event and the bronze in the individual race. In the ensuing months Tom acquired several British titles in uphill races as well as on the flat.

The following year saw Simpson move to France where the sport of cycling was more prominent. During

Figure 2.38.
Tommy Simpson, a cyclist who never gave up.

his first season there he notched up twenty-eight wins. In 1960 he entered the famous Tour de France which covered 2,200 miles in twenty-two days and was renowned as the most gruelling cycle race in the world. Although he did not win he was the youngest of the few riders who finished the race.

In 1961 Tommy entered the Tour of Flanders event and went into the record books as the first Englishman to win this race. A year later he changed clubs and joined Lodeve in the south of France and in 1963 won the Bordeaux to Paris Classic 356 mile non-stop race.

As his success spread demands for him to race in different countries became more prolific. In 1965 he reached the pinnacle of his career when he won the World Championships. However, ill luck intervened the following year when he broke a leg in a skiing accident. He lost a lot of contract money and sponsorships, being unable to compete. During the spring he trained hard to get himself back on top form and resumed competing in the several six-day events. He had success winning a stage of the Tour of Sardinia, becoming the overall winner of Stage 8 of the Paris to Nice Classic and won two stages of the Tour of Spain. Sadly, as part of his plan to achieve fitness, he had been taking various stimulants to drive him on when other competitors' energies were flagging.

He entered the Tour de France in 1967 and on 13 July, on Stage 13, just one kilometre from the summit of Mount Venoux, he died 'in the saddle'. He was asphyxiated, exhausted by the strain placed upon his body by altitude, heat and effort. When he fell from his bike he asked to be put back in the saddle. Even though he was at death's door he would not give in. British sport and international cycling lost one of its greatest heroes on that day. His achievements were remarkable. Tommy Simpson's funeral was attended by cyclists from all over the world paying homage, including a six-times world champion. His grave can be seen in Harworth churchyard (Figure 2.39).

In Loving Memory Of
TOM SIMPSON,
THE DEAR HUSBAND OF HELEN
AND LOVING FATHER OF JANE & JOANNE,
WHO DIED ON MONT VENTOUX, FRANCE
13TH JULY 1967 – AGED 29 YEARS,
WHILST COMPETING WITH THE GREAT BRITAIN TEAM
IN THE TOUR DE FRANCE CYCLE RACE.

HIS BODY ACHED, HIS LEGS GREW TIRED
BUT STILL HE WOULD NOT GIVE IN.

Figure 2.39. Tommy Simpson's grave.

HICKLETON
St Wilfred's churchyard

Several servants' graves can be seen in St Wilfred's churchyard (Figure 2.40). The nearby 'big house', Hickleton Hall (Figure 2.41) is now a Sue Ryder Home but for many years was the residence of Lord and Lady Halifax (Figure 2.42). The following are three examples of inscriptions at a time when 'life in service' was a commonplace occupation for many.

Edward Groom
Departed this life August 1st 1914,
the faithful and attached servant and
friend dear to Lord and Lady Halifax
and all their children

Susan Harris
Departed this life April 17th 1915,
for 43 years a faithful friend of Lord
and Lady Halifax and their children.

Susan Burbridge
Born November 25th 1870 and died
January 15th 1933, for 36 years the
faithful friend and servant of Lord and
Lady Halifax and their family.

Figure 2.40. Hickleton Church in Edwardian times.

Figure 2.41. Hickleton Hall. *Brian Elliott*

MARR, ST HELEN'S CHURCH
Christopher Barker 1529-1599, printer to Queen Elizabeth

The initials 'C.B.' on the pulpit in St Helen's Church (Figure 2.43) are believed to have been carved in recognition of local man and benefactor Christopher Barker who became one of the most important printers of the Elizabethan era. According to Hunter, Barker was born in the vicarage house at Marr and, in addition to the pulpit, erected pews and paved the aisles of the church.

Figure 2.42. Lord Halifax (Edward Frederick Lindley Wood 1881-1959), who was Foreign Secretary 1938-1941.

Figure 2.43. St Helen's Church, Marr.

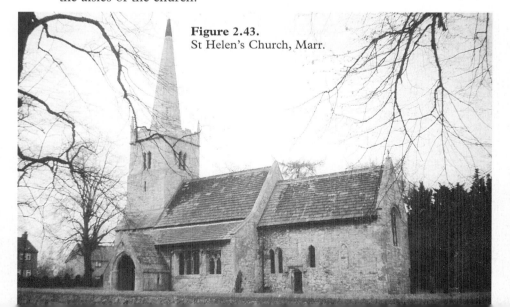

Clemens et Regni moderatrix iusta Britani
Hac forma insigni conspicienda nitet.

Tristia dum gentes circum omnes bella fatigant,
Cæciq; errores toto grassantur in orbe.
Au. Dni pace beas longa, Vera et pietate Britannos: 1579
Iusticia moderans miti sapienter habenas.
Chara domi, celebrisq; foris, longæuaq; regni
Hic teneas, regno tandem fruitura perenni.

Figure 2.44 (left). Title page of an atlas published in 1579, showing Queen Elizabeth seated on the throne and surrounded by allegorical figures.

A former member of the Drapers' Company, Barker was the first to print the Geneva Bible (1575) in England. He went on to purchase the patent for the right to print the Old and New Testaments in English (1577), in effect becoming the queen's printer (Figure 2.44). By 1589 Barker also held the exclusive patent for all state printing including religious books. Altogether he produced thirty-eight editions of the bible between 1575 and 1588. A further thirty-four were produced by his deputies, a really prodigious achievement.

MEXBOROUGH, ST JOHN'S CHURCHYARD
Joel Kirby 1807-1896, temperance movement pioneer

Joel was born in Rotherham on 21 June 1807 but at the age of fourteen was apprenticed to a Barnsley cabinet maker. He married in 1822 and had three sons and three daughters.

After working for a Sheffield firm of cabinet makers he entered into partnership with William and Edwin Peace in their commercial premises in the town. He attended to sales and helped the firm to succeed. Kirby then left to set up in business on his own account, doing so well that he was able to retire at the age of fifty, in 1857.

As a young man, Joel had observed the damage caused by the drinking habits of local people and became an earnest convert to the temperance movement. He helped to design temperance literature and began lecturing on the subject. He was among those who promoted the annual temperance conference held at the Botanical Gardens, Sheffield. At his own expense Kirby had plans drawn up for the Temperance Hall in Town Head Street, Sheffield, and assisted with fund-raising for the building.

At the time, drinking habits were somewhat different than those of today. Beer was strong, cheap and consumed in large quantities.

On his retirement, Joel came to Mexborough and bought the old manor house of Sir William Horne but he could not remain inactive for long and soon became involved in local politics. He was involved in the enclosure of Mexborough Common and was elected as gas inspector and overseer of the poor. He also took an active part in procuring a fire engine for the town (Figure 2.45), raising subscriptions for the project.

Joel served on Mexborough School Board and headed the

Figure 2.45. Mexborough's first purpose-built fire tender inspired by Joel Kirby

enterprise which helped improve the town centre with the building of the Market Hall (Figure 2.46) on land leased from Andrew Montagu. His efforts were appreciated by the townsfolk and Joel was given the honour of performing the official opening of the Hall in 1880. He was also a member of the first burial board, formed to regularise cemetery layout and the provision of public graves. He died on 16 October 1896, aged eighty-nine.

Figure 2.46. The Market Hall at Mexborough, completed in 1880 as the centrepiece of the town. The fire tender was stored in one of the arched rooms to the left hand side of the building.

MEXBOROUGH, CASTLE HILL PARK
William Hackett VC 1873-1916, First World War hero

Sapper W Hackett, 136414 (Figure 2.47), was killed by shell fire on 27 June 1916 near the entrance to a tunnel which he was working on in the Ypres area of Belgium. Earlier, Bill had been awarded the VC for outstanding bravery rescuing several men in an earlier tunnel collapse. At one point he would not leave an injured comrade despite being in imminent danger himself. His citation is shown as Figure 2.48.

> HACKETT, No. 136414, SAPPER WILLIAM.
>
> For most conspicuous bravery when entombed with four others in a gallery owing to the explosion of an enemy mine.
>
> After working for 20 hours a hole was made through fallen earth and broken timber, and the outside party was met. Sapper Hackett helped three of the men through the hole and could easily have followed, but refused to leave the fourth, who had been seriously injured, saying " I am a tunneller ; I must look after the others first."
>
> Meantime the hole was getting smaller, yet he still refused to leave his injured comrade. Finally the gallery collapsed, and though the rescue party worked desperately for four days the attempt to reach the two men failed.
>
> Sapper Hackett, well knowing the nature of sliding earth, and the chances against him, deliberately gave his life for his comrade.— *London Gazette*, 5th August, 1916.

Figure 2.47. Sapper William Hackett VC.

Figure 2.48. Details of Hackett's bravery is shown in the above citation.

During the Great War tunnelling companies were formed as a means of trying to break the stalemate of trench warfare. Bill was in the 254th Tunnelling Company, Royal Engineers at the time of his death. Tunnelling companies in both the Allied and the enemy armies comprised largely of miners who understandably, had the necessary underground skills. The tunnellers fought an horrendous underground war. Sometimes, when opposing tunnellers were digging nearby they would break through into their respective workings and hand-to-hand fighting would break out. Tunnels were dug to plant mines under enemy trench systems, but sometimes they detonated accidentally, killing the diggers. Each side would try to counter-mine the other's tunnels and seek to create cave-ins in order to bury the enemy alive.

Sapper Hackett has no known grave but a fine memorial in his honour can be seen in Mexborough (Figure 2.49). In addition his name is commemorated on the Ploegsteert Memorial in Belgium, some sixteen kilometres south of Ypres. A Mexborough brewery even

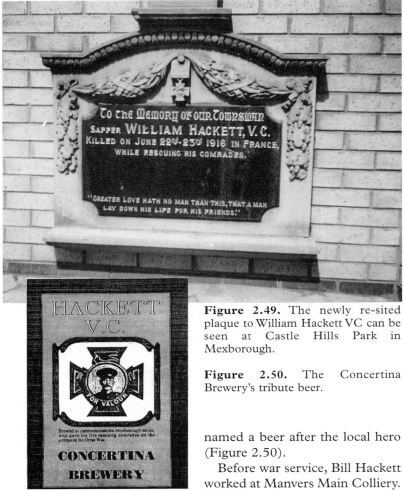

Figure 2.49. The newly re-sited plaque to William Hackett VC can be seen at Castle Hills Park in Mexborough.

Figure 2.50. The Concertina Brewery's tribute beer.

named a beer after the local hero (Figure 2.50).

Before war service, Bill Hackett worked at Manvers Main Colliery. He was forty-three years old when he was killed and left a widow called Alice. His parents were John and Harriet of Nottingham.

PICKBURN
William M Clift 1762-1840, jockey

Clift was born at Wentworth in 1762 and followed his father's occupation as a shepherd. He had first shown interest in horses when working as a farm boy in the village. His riding skills became apparent when he excelled in the pony races held at Wentworth park. The young lad soon came to the notice of Lord Rockingham who

Figure 2.51. Doncaster racecourse and grandstand.
Figure 2.52 (oval). Portrait of William Clift by Harry Hall.

sent him to his racing stables at Swinton, at the side of the *Gate Inn*. Clift later moved to Newmarket, the capital of horse racing in England.

In a remarkable career in which he rode for Lord Rockingham and the Duke of Portland, Clift won a record thirteen classic races including the famous St Leger at Doncaster (Figure 2.51). He also won five Derbys – a record still to be equalled.

William Clift retired from Newmarket to live at Pickburn from where he was accustomed to ride his horse to York for race meetings. He was immortalised on canvas by the London artist Harry Hall, a painting that surfaced at a Christie's auction in June 1996 (Figure 2.52). Clift died aged seventy-eight in 1840.

TICKHILL, ST MARY'S CHURCH
William Fisher 1818-1838, would-be Methodist missionary
A lot had gone through the mind of William Fisher in the cause of the Methodist Church. When he heard about problems in poor parts of the world he decided to devote his life to God and become a missionary in West Africa. The first stage of his journey took him to London where he was to meet up with others and board a ship for the tropics. Unfortunately he became ill and died in London, possibly from cholera.

His gravestone, located to the left of the side entrance to the church (Figure 2.53) has the following details:

> *In memory of William Fisher who having offered*
> *himself as a Wesleyan Missionary to Western Africa*
> *was seized with a painful affliction during the stay*
> *in London which terminated in his death on 2 August*
> *1838 in the 20th year of his life*

Figure 2.53. St Mary's Church, Tickhill. *Brian Elliott*

WADWORTH, ST JOHN'S CHURCH
Edmund (or Esmon) Fitzwilliam c1360-c1430, gentleman
In St John the Baptist Church at Wadworth there are some excellent medieval monuments although they are not all in their original locations. The most impressive survivor is the alabaster monument of Edmund Fitzwilliam and his wife Maud. He is in armour, his head resting on a helmet (bascinet) which has a plume; and he also has a decorated belt which would have supported a sword. His arms are joined in prayer. 'His Lady' has her hands upon her breast and hair finely carved. Her head reclines on a cushion supported by angels holding shields. The monument, drawn and engraved by W. Cowan (Figure 2.54), is used as a plate in Joseph Hunter's *South Yorkshire* (vol.1) and is referred to by Tony Dodsworth and Simeon Bennett in *Aspects of Doncaster 2* (1999).

Figure 2.54. Monument of Edmund Fitzwilliam at Wadworth, from Hunter's *South Yorkshire*, 1828.

Fitzwilliam, who was about seventy years old when he was buried, was the younger son of Sir John Fitzwilliam of Sprotborough who was killed in the reign of Richard II by Richard Spark, a servant of John Aske. His wife, Maud, was the daughter of Sir John Hotham of Holderness. The tomb of their son and heir, Richard Fitzwilliam of Aldwark, knight (d.1497), though unfortunately not well preserved, can be seen in Tickhill Church.

Lionel Copley 1607-1675, early capitalist and ironmaster
There are numerous interesting graves and monuments in St John's

Church at Wadworth (Figure 2.55). Writing in the 1820s, Joseph Hunter referred to the Copley family as 'one of the great ancient families of the West Riding.' Lionel Copley was the youngest son of the family that had lived in a mansion in Wadworth since Elizabethan times. His elder bother, Christopher (whose son had died in 1658), was a colonel who commanded a regiment of mounted troops at the battles of Nantwich and Sherburn in the Civil War. Lionel became sole heir, succeeding to the family estate.

Figure 2.55. St John's Church, Wadworth. *Brian Elliott*

Lionel Copley started his business career well before he took over the estate and already had industrial interests. In 1638 he had been involved in a court case where he was sued for the recovery of £20 in outstanding wage claims by employees in his coal mine. A further case was brought against him at the assizes in 1664 when he was accused of beating one Richard Firth, forcing a bridle into his mouth and then riding around on him for some thirty minutes and repeatedly kicking him.

The earliest mention of Copley's involvement in the iron industry was in 1635 when he was fined for being the owner of iron hammers lying in Marshgate, Doncaster, causing an obstruction on the highway.

With two partners, in 1638, he erected an ironworks at Conisbrough and other forges were built in the Sheffield area, at Ecclesfield and Attercliffe. Copley also had a twenty-five per cent share of an iron forge in the hamlet of Stone, near Tickhill.

In 1655, following a successful application for a patent, he built further ironworks at Bristol and Kingswood Forest. A further forge was taken over at Chapletown. By 1674 the Attercliffe and Wadsley forges alone were generating net profits of £200. Leases were taken out on Rotherham forge, Chapel Furness at Chapletown, Wards End forge, Sheffield and Ecclesfield. When the Chapel Furness and Kimberworth forges were taken over in 1652, Copley paid £2,575 12s 6d for the fixed assets, stock and goodwill. In 1653 a lease was taken out on the three acres of land on which he built what is known as the Rockley Furnace (near Worsbrough, Figure 2.56). The rent was to be £5 per annum with an additional 5s per ton of iron cast, to be paid to Francis Rockley.

Further acquisitions were made of Norton forge and Furness near Sheffield in 1669. In addition Copley operated collieries at Kimberworth and Whiston. These were the biggest pits operating in the area at the time. In an attempt at vertical expansion Copley also operated ironstone mining, therefore controlling the raw materials he needed in his iron production. He also had forestry interests for timber and charcoal requirements.

Figure 2.56. Rockley Furnace

Copley's will is dated 20 November 1675. He died in London seventeen days later. His body was conveyed to Wadworth and interred within the church. Lionel's son, also named Lionel, was educated at Oxford and sought a career in politics, becoming Governor of Hull before going to the American colonies. He was appointed Governor of Maryland in 1655 and died in 1699.

Joseph Hunter transcribed a number of Copley memorials in St John's Church, including,

> *In this place lyes interred the body of*
> *WILLYAM COPLEY Esq., who departed*
> *this life the xx day of May 1658. And of*
> *ANN his wife who dyed the 26th day of*
> *January 1645. And of ELIZABETH COPLEY*
> *the wife of Christopher Copley sonne of*
> *the sayd William and Ann who dyed the*
> *16th day of August 1644. This stone was*
> *layed here at the charge of Lyonell Copley*
> *the younger sonne of of the said William*
> *and Ann the 28th day of Aprill 1660*

> *Here lyeth the body of LIONELL COPLEY Esq.,*
> *died the 7 day of December 1675. Here also*
> *lyeth the body of CASTILLA daughter of the*
> *said Lionell Copley. She was first married to*
> *John Beckworth of Sleningford in the county*
> *of York Esq., and had issue one son and two*
> *daughters, and afterwards to the Rev. Tho.*
> *Maulyverer rector of Sprodborough [sic]:and*
> *died the 13 of May 1700 deservedly lamented*
> *by all that knew her.*

> *Here lyeth the body of FRIZALINA COPLEY*
> *the wife of Lionell Copley Esq., who departed*
> *this life the 6 day November in the year of our*
> *Lord 1696, and in the 86th year of her age.*

THE ROTHERHAM AREA

The environs of Rotherham are pleasant and picturesque. On an eminence... stands an elegant mansion, belonging to the Walker family; and in the neighbourhood... is situated Wentworth House, the magnificent residence of Earl Fitzwilliam

From Edward Baines' *Directory of the West Riding* (1822)

Figure 3.1. Old Wentworth Church in winter. *Brian Elliott*

FIRBECK, ST PETER'S CHURCH
Sir Ralph Knight 1621-1691, a leading officer in the Parliamentary Army

St Peter's was built in c1820, with later additions but memorials from its medieval predecessor were described in some detail by antiquarians and historians, including Joseph Hunter who was quite impressed that family memorials had not been 'utterly destroyed' as was the case in other examples. The new church had been funded by Mrs Gally-Knight with the help of the society for building and enlarging churches.

The Knights came from Newbury in Berkshire, but after Sir Ralph acquired an estate at Langold he soon purchased the nearby Letwell estate, living at Langold. Later, he bought an estate at Firbeck, of which he was particularly fond and then adopted the house there as his principal seat.

Ralph, at the age of twenty-three, enlisted into the Parliamentary Army when the Civil War broke out. In October 1643 he was in service as a sergeant-major, and was distinguished for his leadership during the fight for Horncastle. He was also ordered to march on the castle at Bolingbroke. Popular with the troops, Ralph was somewhat critical of his fellow officers. On 23 June 1646 he married Faith Dickinson, daughter of the late vicar of Rotherham, in Rotherham parish church.

Ralph continued in the army throughout the Commonwealth period and in 1658 was in Scotland as a major in General George Monck's regiment. After Richard Cromwell (Oliver's son) resigned as Lord Protector, Monck (Figure 3.2) consulted with his brother, Reverend Nicholas Monck and Major Knight. Monck's army was not ready to march into England for at least six weeks, so Knight was sent with four troops

Figure 3.2. General George Monck, 1608-1670

of horseguard and six companies of infantry to surprise the Earl of Newcastle who was attempting to take over the day-to-day affairs of the nation. General Monck, however, changed his mind and sent word to Knight rescinding the order and to make camp at Alnwick.

Monck appointed Knight and Lieutenant Colonel Clobery to act as his commissioners to commence negotiating for the restoration of Parliament's authority. A meeting was proposed with General Lambert and his forces at York, but Lambert had thrown in his lot with General Fleetwood in London and therefore was unable to enter into any discussions for the time being. Lambert commanded a force of 12,000 men while Monck's army was only 6,000 strong, though very loyal.

Knight and Clobery left Lambert and proceeded to London to meet Fleetwood's commissioners where they agreed and signed a document continuing to oppose Charles Stuart's right to the throne and reasserting the authority of Parliament. The General Council was to summon Parliament as soon as possible and the armies, by then milling round in the political confusion, were to return to their bases and resume their duties of defending the realm and keeping the peace.

Knight and Clobery signed the statement on 15 November 1658 and returned to Scotland where they found Monck dissatisfied with the terms and unwilling to concur with them. Out of affection for Knight he blamed neither of his commissioners for the agreement he thus aborted.

Monck devised a new strategy, promoting Knight to colonel, placing him in command of three regiments and sent him to Morpeth, with orders also to capture Newcastle. Knight achieved this with ease while Monk began his march to London. Monck paused at York to be joined by Fairfax and other Yorkshire gentry pledged support. He continued, staying at Knight's house in Langold on 19 January 1659. The colonel rode down from Newcastle to act as host and accompanied Monck on the southward march.

The army increased in numbers as it progressed towards London, with officers sympathetic to Monck's cause and command. A large force of 5,800, for example, joined at Nottingham. When the army reached the capital the various regiments were strategically camped around London.

In the meantime Parliament met and offered the title of 'Commissioner' to Monck and a new Parliament was summoned. Its successes depended on support from the armies and each colonel was made responsible for collecting signatures of support. Knight used his influence and obtained the consent of his officers. The outcome was the election of a new Parliament and the process towards the restoration of the monarchy in the person of Charles II.

Figure 3.3. Charles II landing at Dover after his restoration. In appreciation of the support of Ralph Knight, the latter was duly knighted.

In appreciation of the role he played, the new king knighted Colonel Knight and bestowed other favours on him (Figure 3.3).

When it was felt that the disputes were over and that the country was finally at peace with itself the colonels were directed to disband their regiments. Sir Ralph received his order on 13 August 1667, at Yarmouth.

As a figure of influence in the affairs of the nation Sir Ralph Knight was frequently visited by the most powerful men of the day, calling on him at his Langold estate.

The inscription (translated from Latin) on the memorial to Ralph Knight's wife, Fain, reads as follows:

Most sweet wife of Ralph Knight, Horseman of
Laughall (Langold), who after 23 years happily
married, the month of 25 days added on, of
happy childbirth, had 15 children, happily

carried through 43 years of life with an
esteemed husband, sweet children, their love
happy in poverty and in the pleasant
neighbourhood where no one, unless wicked,
was separate, among the nobility. The
sweetest God, far away, closed the day
fatefully at the right time for him, too early
for us alas, then end 18th April AD 1671.
God gave them his servants and their children.

Figure 3.4. St. Thomas' Church, Kilnhurst.. *Brian Elliott*

Figure 3.5. Memorial to Kilnhurst Colliery workers.

KILNHURST, ST THOMAS' CHURCH
Thomas Astill 1854-1874, Warren Vale Colliery disaster victim

A number of victims of mining accidents and disasters are buried in St Thomas' churchyard at Kilnhurst (Figure 3.4). Today, a commemorative half winding wheel and a memorial bear witness to the ultimate price of coal (Figure 3.4).

Warren Vale Colliery was situated between Swinton and Rawmarsh on what is now the site of the council tip (Figure 3.6). The first shaft was sunk in the 1830s. The colliery was owned by J. and J. Charlesworth who were always careful to ensure that their pits were worked to the highest safety standards. Even so, in December 1851 fifty men and boys were killed in an explosion of methane gas.

Figure 3.6. Site of Warren Vale Colliery.

On the morning of 20 November 1874, 148 men and 38 boys descended the pit and all was well. At 8.00a.m. the fire trier, John Warrington, completed his gas tests. The air was good and there was no indication of the disaster that was to follow.

The colliery had three shafts with workings extending in different directions. Part of the mine was known as the Rawmarsh Pit where the shaft was 180 yards deep and workings ran under the old village of Swinton. The men were currently working a mile and a half from the bottom in an area called the South Level and in the Barnsley Silkstone seam. At 8.10a.m. Tom Harrison, the weighman, noticed a considerable quantity of dust rising from the pit shaft. He raised the alarm immediately, fearing an explosion had occurred. Although no sound had been heard at the colliery the blast under Swinton had been tremendous as the force of the explosion ripped along the underground passages.

As news spread, help was rushed to the pithead. Local doctors, Lord Fitzwilliam's mining agent and mining engineers among many others risked their lives to assist in the rescue. Wailing wives and children gathered at the pithead waiting for news of their husbands, fathers and sons and the police had to be called to keep the crowd back. Rescue parties descended the shaft and the first body was recovered at 10.30a.m. By 3.30pm in the afternoon thirteen bodies had been recovered. The last one was brought to the surface after 5.00p.m. Volunteers worked until they were exhausted and their places were taken by others. Medical treatment was given to the survivors (Figure 3.7).

It was believed that the explosion came about when a section of coal was removed, releasing a compact pocket of methane gas. As the air was tested 'clear' ten minutes before there could be no other explanation for the suddenness. The colliery worked the old stall and pillar system of coal removal. The pillars were left to hold the roof while the coal was extracted. Naked lights were still used in the pit and were the source of the ignition of the gas. Some of the positions of the victims suggested they were having a breakfast break. Of the persons in the South Level, all but five lost their lives. Although the

Figure 3.7. The injured being attended.

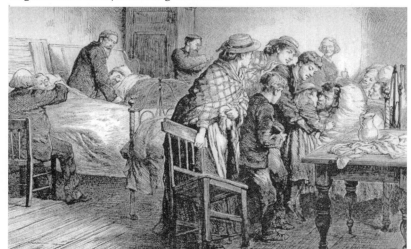

five were working well away from the seat of the explosion they were burnt by the blast.

The accident resulted in twenty-one deaths, details (including dependents) as follows:

George Taylor, collier, Rawmarsh, wife and four children
John Walker, trammer, Kilnhurst, single
Joseph Thompson, horse driver, Upper Haugh, a boy
Richard Skelton, collier, Rawmarsh, wife and seven children
Thomas Beighton, trammer, Swinton, single
Thomas Astill, collier, Meadow Works, Rawmarsh, wife and four children
James Morte, collier, Rawmarsh, wife and three children
Benjamin Taylor, trammer, Rawmarsh, wife and two children
George Wright, collier, Rawmarsh, wife and one child
Samuel Tomlinson, collier, Swinton, wife and four children
Samuel Skelton, horse driver, Rawmarsh, wife and five children
Isaac and Luke Oxley (brothers), colliers, of Newhill, single
Henry Stead, collier, Swinton, wife and two children
John Tomlinson, collier, Rawmarsh, wife and four children
William Byrom, collier, Four Lanes, Rawmarsh, wife and four children
Thomas Roberts, packer, Rawmarsh, wife and four children
John Wooding, trammer, Wath (recently married)
John Jowitt, collier, Swinton, wife and three children
Frederick Cliffe, trammer, Kilnhurst, single
George King, collier, Kilnhurst, single

KILNHURST CEMETERY

Charles (Chuck) William Bentham 1891-1916, Somme victim

Private Bentham (CW 23201) enlisted in the 8th Service Battalion of the York and Lancaster Regiment in Wath. Before the war he was a miner at Kilnhurst and a keen local footballer.

Bentham was mortally wounded on the terrible first day of the Battle of the Somme 1 July 1916, one of the blackest days in the history of the British Army. At 7.30a.m. the 8th Yorks and Lancs advanced with many other regular, territorial and Kitchener battalions into unbroken barbed wire and the muzzles of German machine guns. The British troops were ordered to advance at walking pace as it was believed that the opposing forces would have been destroyed by the previous artillery bombardment (Figure 3.8). This was a fatal mistake. Casualties suffered by the British, some 60,000, bore bloody witness to the high command's lack of intelligence.

Figure 3.8. British troops bombarding with an eighteen pounder filed gun at the Somme in 1916.

Chuck's battalion sustained more than its fair share of casualties than any unit which participated on the first day of the Somme offensive. Their jump-off position was near the village of Authuille in a section of the line called 'The Nab', a dog-leg of trench line which exposed the battalion to fire from the front and side.

Most of Chuck's comrades lie buried at 'Blighty Valley' cemetery near Authuille. But he was picked up from the field by stretcher-

Figure 3.9. The wounded being attended after the first day of the Somme.

bearers. Under the military system he would then have been taken to the nearest regimental aid post where the most rudimentary treatment and dressings would have been applied (Figure 3.9). Next, the wounded were taken back to a casualty clearing station where more thorough attention was given. Those who survived this far were then transferred by road, rail, canal or on foot to a much larger base hospital well distant from the front line.

Obviously after such a disaster, the army's medical services were overwhelmed by the volume of casualties. The wounded were sent back to Britain as soon as possible, to relieve the strain of field hospitals. Chuck was sent to a military hospital in Wrexham. His wife, Amy, and their four-year -old son, Bill, were able to visit him. They took him some black grapes (a rare luxury then) which he was able to eat. But he died of his wounds on 23 July 1916, aged twenty-five. Amy was able to have his body returned by train to Kilnhurst for interment. Chuck's son, Bill Bentham, became chairman of Swinton UDC during the 1950s.

Bentham's grave can be found just inside the gate of the cemetery, on the left side. There is no reference to his war service on the stone but his name is inscribed on the Kilnhurst war memorial a few feet away.

KIMBERWORTH, ST THOMAS'S CHURCHYARD (Figure 3.10)
John Brookes 1865-1884, steelworker killed at work

His grave can be located by going round the church (from the main entrance) and towards a large brown granite monument. The grave is

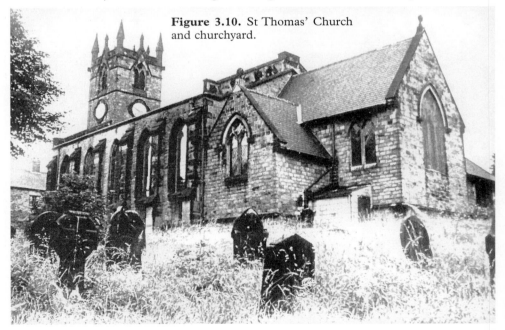

Figure 3.10. St Thomas' Church and churchyard.

about five metres away, the inscription reads as follows:

> *Affectionate remembrance of John Brookes,*
> *second son of David and Suzanna Allen, who*
> *was severely burned through the turning over*
> *of a ladle of molten steel at Phoenix Works,*
> *Rotherham, September 9th and died on*
> *September 10th 1884, aged 19 years*

The Phoenix Works opened in 1830 and cast large forgings for ships and trams etc. In 1818 Phoenix operated as a partnership between Charles Sandford and William Owen. The company designed a new type of railway wheel which was shown at the Great Exhibition of 1851. After expansion, the company fell on hard times and was liquidated in 1872. In 1875 the premises were taken over and production resumed, but the above inscription certainly shows that working in the steel industry could be one of the more dangerous of occupations.

Maltby, Grange Cemetery (new section)
Sir John (Jack) Layden 1926-96, JP, Leader of Rotherham MBC

Sir 'Jack' (he preferred this name to John) died on 28 May 1996, aged 70, while on a family holiday in Blackpool. He had stepped down from Rotherham MBC earlier that month after forty-three years in local government (Figure 3.11)

Jack had gone straight down the pit when he left school at the age of fourteen and remained a working miner until he was made redundant in 1986. He was a leading member of the National Union of Mineworkers in the Yorkshire area for many years.

His service in local government began in 1953 when he was elected for the west ward of Maltby Urban District Council. He continued to represent the same ward until May 1996. Jack was appointed a Justice of the Peace in 1964.

During his years in politics Maltby merged with other authorities to form Rotherham Metropolitan Council in 1974. Jack was elected as leader of the new authority and continued in

Figure 3.11.
Sir Jack Layden

Figure 3.12. Sir Jack and Lady Layden outside Buckingham Palace.

office until his retirement.

In 1974 he joined the policy committee of the newly formed Association of Metropolitan Authorities, becoming Chairman in 1984 and served until 1991. In 1977 he was appointed to the Yorkshire and Humberside Economic Planning Council.

Jack's interests were wide and ranged from chairing South Yorkshire Police Authority (until the end of 1995) to being a director of Rotherham Football Club. He rarely missed an opportunity to refer in his 'speeches' to 'his' football club.

An intense involvement with and loyalty to his own folk was extended to include his dealings regionally, nationally and internationally, too. His philosophy was to do as much as he could for as many as he could. One of his proudest memories was of receiving a knighthood in 1988 (Figure 3.12).

During a long political career he met Pope Paul II, President Gorbachov of the USSR, President Reagan of the USA, and all British prime ministers from Sir Winston Churchill to John Major. One happy memory was his visit to

Figure 3.13. The *Sir Jack* public house, near Morrison's supermarket, on the A631 at Bramley.

10 Downing Street to see Mrs Thatcher. He 'put her straight' on a few matters and claimed to be one of the few to call Margaret 'love' – and live to tell the tale!

Sir Jack was made an Honorary Citizen of Indianapolis and granted the Freedom of the City of London.

As an accomplished cornet player in the Maltby Miners' Band in his younger days, he continued to be very fond of brass bands. Recently a new public house, *Sir Jack*, was named in his honour (Figure 3.13).

MASBOROUGH CEMETERY
Thomas Uttley Brookes 1870-1886, killed at Bessemer Steelworks

The young man's gravestone is inscribed

Accidentally killed at
the Bessemer Steelworks,
Ickles, October 26th 1886,
aged 16 years

The Bessemer Steel Works was founded fourteen years earlier to incorporate the synonymous new process and by 1879 some 2,750 ingots were being produced each week. Trading difficulties then arose and various partnerships were formed to carry on the business. The site was absorbed into the Steel Tozer and Hampton Company Limited and then continued casting into the twentieth century.

Thomas Brookes, whilst on the night shift, was instructed to take a

Figure 3.14. Steel Cutting machine.

steel cobble (or lump) down to the new shears (Figure 3.14) in order to have it cut into four lengths. Unfortunately the lad decided to go to the old shears, saving his legs. These were not working, so he turned on the steam that powered the machine himself, despite no previous direct operational experience. While the pressure was building up Thomas tried to move the fly-wheel to start the motor.

Suddenly, the wheel jerked into action and Thomas was dragged over it and dropped into the cogs which operated the cutters. His screams were heard and assistance soon arrived and the machine stopped. It had to be restarted and put into reverse in order to free Thomas' leg and abdomen from the cogs, but nothing could be done for the lad and he died.

At the inquiry Mr William Eckersley, the chief engineer, described the position of the engine and explained that it was the usual practice to start the fly-wheel with a rod and not by hand. To reach the wheel Thomas must have climbed through the guard fence. His colleagues said they had never known him disobey an order before. He had always been a good, stout worker despite his youth.

Neri Poundall 1873-1898, miner killed by a rock fall

Great mining disasters understandably hit the news headlines but many more miners were injured or lost their lives in underground haulage accidents and in roof falls. A noteworthy example can be seen by reference to the inscription on the gravestone of Neri Poundall,

The beloved Husband of Selina Poundall
who was killed at Rotherham Main
Colliery by a fall of rock measuring 19
feet in length, 4 feet wide,
eighteen inches thick,
died December 29th 1898 aged 25 years
A sudden change in moment fell, I had
not the time to bid my friends farewell,
think not strange, death happens on to all,
today was mine, tomorrow you will fall.

Rotherham Main Colliery (Figure 3.15) was sunk in 1890 by John Brown and Co, the Sheffield steelmakers. The pit was situated alongside the river Rother near Canklow. It ceased production in 1954.

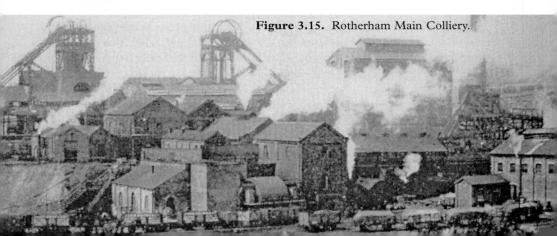

Figure 3.15. Rotherham Main Colliery.

RAWMARSH, ST MARY'S CHURCHYARD
Edward Calvert d.1874, killed after getting lost in the pit

Edward Calvert of Rawmarsh was newly recruited to work at the Warren Vale Colliery (Figures 3.16-17). On 24 March 1874 he entered and descended the shaft and was instructed to take some light materials to another part of the mine. He was asked if he knew the way and stated that he did. However, Mr Dodson, a pit deputy, took the precaution of explaining the route and drawing a map. Calvert set off at 8.20a.m. At 9.00a.m a juvenile reported to Charles Moore, the fire trier that he had noticed some brickwork had been dislodged by an explosion. He had continued through the gate and heard moaning. They found Edward Calvert who had taken the brunt of the blast and was very badly hurt.

Calvert was carried out of the mine virtually unconscious and died

Figure 3.16. View down Warren Vale towards Rawmarsh, the colliery is on the left-hand side of the road.

Figure 3.17. Early view of Rawmarsh with St Mary's Church at the top of the hill.

of his injuries shortly afterwards. Apparently he had lost and entered the older parts of the mine, carrying a naked light. The colliery had notorious gas problems and parts of the mine where Calvert was fatally injured were scheduled to be sealed off the following day.

Rotherham, Boston Cemetery
Children killed in runaway motor tragedy, 1909

Samuel Houghton (aged five), Laura Steel (six), Doris Braisford (six) and Amy Myers (six) lost their lives on 15 September 1909. Their grave is quite distinctive and can be seen on the right with one's back to the War Memorial, at the entrance to the cemetery (Figure 3.18).

Mr Fuller Ward had brought four tons of bricks from the Midland Iron Company's works at Masborough and was taking them to Middle Lane. At 4.00p.m. he turned his steam-driven lorry and

trailer into St Ann's Road (Figure 3.19). The total weight of the vehicle was almost nine tons. The lorry was near the top of the incline when it slipped out of gear and began rolling back.

The children at St Ann's Council School were leaving for home unaware the vehicle was rolling out of control towards them. The assistant driver, William Hunt, jumped out of the cab and threw bricks under the wheels in a desperate effort to reduce speed but the lorry continued to proceed at about 20mph. A steam lorry would have been virtually silent and any sound it may have made would have been unnoticed in the chatter and laughter of 300 children

Figure 3.18. Memorial to four children killed by a steam lorry, 15 September 1909.

Figure 3.19. A steam lorry being loaded.

dashing out of school unaware of the approaching danger.

A large group of children were clustered at the corner of St Leornard's Road (Figure 3.20) by the entrance gates to St Stephen's Church. Mr Ward tried to steer the vehicle round the corner into St Leornard's Road in the hope that the rise there would slow it down but the lorry curved wider than he anticipated and crushed some of the infants against the wall and iron railings. The lives of three little

Figure 3.20. The scene of the accident today.

girls and a boy were tragically ended. They were from working families in the neighbourhood with brothers and sisters and the community was stricken with grief.

A public subscription was initiated by the Mayor of Rotherham, Councillor Mullins, in order to erect a memorial to the children. They are buried together beneath a stone which gives details of the tragedy and is surmounted by a statue of an angelic child.

ROTHERHAM (EAST DENE)
Cholera Burial Ground

A small burial ground located between two properties on Park Road, East Dene, serves as a reminder of the terrible 'plague' that struck many parts of Britain in 1831-32 and again in 1848 (Figure 3.21). In the first outbreak more than 50,000 people died, most from the poorer classes of society where sanitary conditions were very bad, thus aiding the spread of the water-borne disease. The first symptoms were vomiting and diarrhoea. Excruciating cramps occurred in the calves of the legs, thighs and abdomen. The victims took on a blue, sunken complexion and had cold, clammy sweats. The voice became husky and within a short space of time most of those affected would collapse into a coma, usually with fatal consequences. Industrial working-class areas where families lived in cramped conditions and in close proximity to one another suffered dreadfully when cholera struck.

It was common practice – because of the highly contagious nature of the disease – for cholera victims to be buried together, in a separate burial ground, away from the town. In 1832 the Rotherham example was thus sited in countryside well away from the

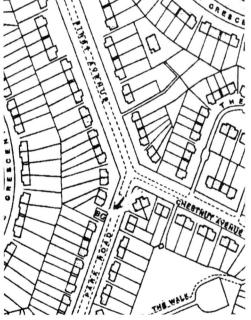

Figure 3.21. Map showing the location of the Cholera Burial Ground off Park Road, East Dene.

Figure 3.22. The Cholera Burial Ground today.

edge of the town and kept 'out of sight' by means of a high brick enclosure. The removal of the latter and subsequent suburban housing development has made the site even less conspicuous (Figure 3.22) but, when visited, this 'little plot of land' is a grim reminder of an epidemic that ruined the lives of many local families.

1832 Outbreak

William Holmer	30 August
Martin Robinson	30 August
Thomas Ellis	30 August
James Scott	31 August
Esther Pashley	31 August
Mary Hodgson	5 September
A stranger	11 September
Joshua Jenkinson	20 September
Joseph Cundy	1 October
Elizabeth Lee	1 October
– Hobson	2 October
Sarah Crowder	2 October
Charlotte Lee	2 October
Ann Woodger	4 October
Richard Pool	4 October
Mary Hudson	6 October
James Calton	7 October
Charlotte Round	9 October
Joseph Woodhead	14 October

William Mile	14 October
Askham Eyre	18 October
James Peace	18 October

1849 Outbreak

Joseph Goldsborough	16 September
James Ellis	27 October
Dr John Holmes	29 October
Michael Bradshaw	29 October
William Carmichael	31 October
Charles Jackson	1 November
Hannah Cottam	2 November
Ann Bayliffe	2 November

At the height of epidemics, it was thought that infected corpses would contaminate the soil, thus aiding the spread of the disease, so 'isolated' burial was thought to be the safest practice.

Figure 3.23. Harry Crossley, British Cruiserweight champion of 1929.

SWINTON, ST MARGARET'S CHURCHYARD
Harry Crossley 1904-1948, British Cruiserweight boxing champion

Harry (Figure 3.23) lived in Queen Street, Swinton. Like his brother, Herbert, he was a powerfully built youth. Interested in boxing, both lads trained at the *Plant Hotel*, Mexborough. When Herbert suddenly died following a fight in New York, on 20 August 1924, Harry also decided to pursue a career in boxing, trying to emulate his famous brother who had achieved the title of British Heavyweight Novice Champion five years earlier.

Harry Crossley's first fight was on 24 July 1924, against Cyril Divine of Mexborough. He won on points and went on to take part in a further fifty-six contests, and then a fight for the British Cruiserweight crown when on 25 November 1929 he fought Frank Moody. The fight lasted the full fifteen rounds and was a gruelling match, but Harry managed to take the title on points. Afterwards he fought on another

Figure 3.24. Unveiling of a wall plaque dedicated to the Crossley brothers by his daughters, with Giles Brearley on the right

thirty-five occasions until retirement, on 26 March 1934. He only lost eighteen fights in a ten year career.

After retirement, Harry became a publican in the Midlands, finally settling in Stamford, Lincolnshire, where he died in 1948.

A plaque in Queen Street, Swinton, was recently unveiled in honour of the remarkable sporting achievements of Herbert and Harry Crossley (Figure 3.24).

Harry's grave can be seen by entering the churchyard through the main gate and taking the path to the right. Continue to the churchyard extension and the grave is located on the right.

William Llandeg 1809-1836, pottery artist

William Llandeg joined the Rockingham pottery at an early age. He is included in the Swinton militia list for 1829 and 1831. His name often appears in the Rockingham pattern book and he became noted for the raspberry or blackberry border which he so intricately painted onto various pieces of porcelain. It was sometimes used as a border for his own designs. He died in October 1836 aged only twenty-seven, sadly missed by the pottery but his work lives on.

Rockingham pottery and porcelain are now sought after throughout the world and are very

Figure 3.25. A fine piece of decorated Rockingham pottery

Figure 3.26. The Rockingham pottery 'Waterloo' kiln is now a listed monument

collectable. The pottery closed in 1842 and surviving examples of his work are highly valued (Figures 3.25 and 3.26).

Sydney Bell 1921-40, first Swinton resident killed in the Second World War

Private Sydney Bell, 474660 (Figure 3.27), was a territorial soldier in the Hallamshire Battalion of the York and Lancaster Regiment. Much of his training was carried out at the Regimental Drill Hall at the rear of Wath-upon-Dearne swimming baths, now a clothing factory. He was a signal and telegraph engineer with the LNER Company in the Mexborough area. He was a keen cyclist and swimmer and, according to many of his family who still live in the area, a friendly and likable young man.

After mobilisation the Hallamshire Battalion became part of the 146th Infantry Brigade which was sent on the ill-fated Norwegian Campaign early in 1940 (Figure 3.28). The Hallamshire escaped the brunt of the fighting although they had to dodge a number of attacks from the air, the last of which caused the only fatalities suffered by the battalion during the retreat from Norwegian waters. Being forced to leave most of their equipment behind, the men of the Hallamshire, along with other regiments and some French troops, were evacuated by sea from the coast of Norway.

The Luftwaffe launched furious attacks on the transport ships, later turning their attention to the destroyer escorts. The Tribal Class *HMS Alfridi* carried men of the Hallams. The French *Bison* was hit. Oil poured from her and more men died in the

Figure 3.27. Private Sydney Bell.

Figure 3.28. View of the British fleet carrying out the troop evacuation of Norway.

flames on the water than from enemy fire. *Alfridi* stayed behind to pick up survivors and after circling *Bison* for two hours had to sink her. Before she caught up with the rest of the convoy she herself was hit by a bomb on the forecastle mess just as some of the men were having their lunch. Thirteen of the Hallamshire Battalion, including Sydney Bell, lost their lives and several others were injured. Many made narrow escapes by climbing through the hole in the ship's side. The destroyer sank in twenty minutes at about 13.45 hours on 3 May 1940.

Sydney Bell was just nineteen years old and the wreck of *HMS Alfridi* is regarded as his and his comrades' war grave. His name can be viewed on Swinton War Memorial (Figure 3.29) and on the Brookwood Memorial (to those who were lost at sea) in Surrey.

Reverend Hugh Quarrell BA 1902-1962, vicar of Swinton

Hugh Quarrell (Figure 3.30) was vicar of St Margaret's at Swinton (Figure 3.31) for twenty years from 1942. His sudden death

Figure 3.29.
Swinton War Memorial

Figure 3.30. Reverend Hugh Quarrell outside St Margaret's Church.

in a Dublin street while on holiday in 1962 came as a great shock and caused much sorrow in the Swinton area. He was aged sixty.

During his incumbency he conducted many baptisms, marriages and funerals as well as preparing dozens of folk for confirmation. He therefore touched the lives of many Swinton residents.

In 1954 Hugh published *A History of Swinton* (Figure 3.32). The local committee involved in planning the 1951 Festival of Britain celebrations invited him to produce the book. Reverend Quarrell spent much time and effort in the collection of information for his history and the

Figure 3.31. St Margaret's, Swinton, from an old postcard.
Figure 3.32. Title page from Hugh's '*History*', published in 1954.

book remains an excellent source for local historians and schools.

Quarrell's grave can be seen near the vicarage field wall, beyond the east window of the church.

THRYBERGH, ST LEONARD'S CHURCH
William Lilley, gamekeeper killed by poachers in 1865

Part of the lands adjacent to Thrybergh was owned by a wealthy Rotherham solicitor who had a keen interest in shooting and field sports. He employed four gamekeepers to manage his estate. In the nineteenth century poaching was considered to be a very serious crime and, as the powerful gentry had influence over local magistrates, the punishments meted out to convicted offenders were quite harsh. The crime was regarded as a personal attack against the landholder.

William Sykes of Midland Road in Mexborough, a puddler at the Masborough forge, ran a poaching syndicate for which he was notorious. On 10 October 1865 he rendezvoused with six others he had recruited at Carr House Colliery (Figure 3.33). They passed by the railway line and the canal and on to Dalton and Thrybergh where they set their rabbit nets (Figure 3.34) on land near Blacking Mill. They worked the field with their dogs but with little success.

Figure 3.33. Carr House Colliery.

Sykes decided to move on to the more prolific Silverwood Estate. William Lilley had anticipated the raid and, with three other gamekeepers, lay in wait between Silverwood and the seed fields. As Sykes and his gang approached the gamekeepers challenged them

Figure 3.34. A rabbit snare.

but they were outnumbered. After a vicious fight (Figure 3.35) Lilley was left unconscious and, within hours, dead.

After twenty-one days of police investigation and the offer of a £350 reward, Sykes was arrested and, on 21 December 1865, taken to Leeds Assizes for trial. One of the gang, to save his own skin, turned queen's evidence against Sykes and his co-defendants. The judge expressed his astonishment when the jury acquitted two of the gang and found Sykes and his three

Figure 3.35. Poachers and gamekeepers clash

companions in crime, guilty of the lesser charge of manslaughter. In his summing up he had leaned towards a clear case of murder.

William Sykes was sentenced to penal servitude for life and his three fellow criminals each received twenty years' imprisonment.

John Whittaker, farmer and cattle dealer murdered in 1856.
John Whittaker was a gentleman farmer who dealt in cattle and sheep. On 16 October 1856, he set off to York to buy sheep at the livestock fair there, carrying £300 in cash. The stock available on the day was not entirely to his satisfaction, so he did not buy all his requirement. He had arranged for his servant to meet him on his return at Swinton railway station with a horse and gig but, as his business in York had delayed him longer than anticipated, he could only get a later train which took him to Rotherham. He arrived there at 11o'clock at night.

Figure 3.36. Dalton Brook today. Whittaker was attacked at the spot where the traffic lights now stand.

He decided that rather than risk travelling in the dark it would be more prudent to spend the night at the *Wheatsheaf Hotel* and journey on to Thrybergh in the morning. The hotel was closed and the landlord could not be roused so Whittaker called at the *Packhorse Inn* for refreshment. Perhaps he over-indulged and clouded his judgement, for he then decided to walk back to Thrybergh.

As he approached Dalton Brook (Figure 3.36) he heard voices behind him which were getting nearer and louder. He passed the *Grapes Tavern* and started up the hill. As he looked back he could make out the figures of four men coming closer. Whittaker turned back down the hill to be nearer the *Grapes* and the neighbouring blacksmith's shop where he would feel more secure if the need should arise. The four men intercepted him, beat him up, hit him over the head with a truncheon, robbed him of the £180 he still had with him and left him for dead in a pool of blood at the roadside.

Half-blinded with blood from his head wounds, Whittaker managed to drag himself to the nearest house and raise the alarm. It was now 1o'clock in the morning.

The constable was sent for from Rawmarsh but Whittaker, unaware of the serious nature of his injuries, stated that he wished to go back to Rotherham as he was anxious the police should capture the robbers quickly. He was in no fit condition to do so and was allowed home with a servant on a cart on the understanding that he was accompanied by an armed man.

Mr Blythman, a surgeon from Swinton, attended John but his injuries were so severe and he had lost so much blood that there was nothing that could be done.

The verdict at the inquest held on 31 October was 'wilful murder be person or persons unknown'. John Whittaker's family put up a reward of £200 for information leading to the conviction of the murderers, but to no avail.

In 1857 a stone with the initials 'J.W.' and the date '1856' was placed near the blacksmith's shop on the roadside to mark the exact spot where the murder had taken place. The stone remained there until the 1950s when it was removed for road-widening.

Sir John Reresby 1634-1689, gentleman, of Thrybergh Hall

Sir John was born on 14 April 1634, in the great bedchamber at Thrybergh Hall. He was an adventurous and mischievous child and at the age of three fell out of an upstairs window. He broke a thigh which left him with a slight limp. Nevertheless he still took part in active sports, was a good horseman and an accomplished dancer. Sir John's childhood years were spent at Thrybergh where he was taught by a private tutor. At fifteen he was sent away to London to broaden his education. His mother took a keen interest in his affairs after the death of his father when John was twelve. He attended the Blew House School and later passed the entrance examination for Cambridge University. He fell out with the university authorities because they did not appear to treat him with the deference to which he felt his noble status entitled him. So he took himself off on a 'grand tour of Europe'. He enjoyed the experience so much that he adapted to European ways and stayed away until 1660 when he returned to England permanently to claim his inheritance and administer the family estate.

John's mother had done her best to manage the estate in his absence but had found the task difficult. She allowed him an income of £40 per annum from the rents but he found he could not well maintain his European lifestyle on so little income. While he had been abroad he had become fluent in Italian, French, German and Dutch. He was small in stature but blessed with courage and could be aggressive when pressed. He learnt to resort to litigation rather than force to settle problems, acknowledging that the pen was mightier than the sword. As the lord of the manor he was often asked to resolve problems regarding disputed rights of way, fishing rights on local waters and family quarrels, among other matters.

He was a compulsive diarist and recorded events of the late Stuart period probably more than any other writer. A man of many talents, the English nobility at large looked down upon Sir John as deficient in the finer points of aristocratic demeanour.

Figure 3.37. Thomas Osborne, Earl of Danby a friend and neighbour of Sir John Reresby. Danby lived at Kiveton Hall.

When he returned to his estate one of the first tasks he set about was to repair the damage left by the Civil War. He found it in a dreadful condition. He was made a justice of the peace and Sheriff of Yorkshire. Reresby made time to listen to petitioners and if he believed they had a genuine case he would make every effort to ensure they had the support they needed. In one example, he won the esteem of the cutlers of Sheffield by fighting for the abolition of a hearth tax which would have ruined their trade and livelihood.

As a young man he entered politics under the patronage of the Duke of Buckingham but the two men fell out over slights about each other's courage and integrity. In his capacity as Sheriff of Yorkshire Sir John issued a warrant for Buckingham's arrest. He became associated with the 'rival faction' in Yorkshire led by the Earl of Burlington.

When Buckingham was restored to royal favour, Sir John was stripped of all his public offices and retired to his estate and local affairs. He left national politics alone for eight years.

In 1673 an election was in the air and Sir John successfully stood for a vacant seat against the Duke of Buckingham. He was very friendly with the Earl of Danby (Figure 3.37) and moved once more into political prominence. On 10 May 1682, he was sworn in as Military Governor of York and as chief justice of the peace for the city. He had frequent access to Charles II and James II for consultation. They bestowed on him the right to raise troops as a Regimented Company which could consist of 100 men, one lieutenant, one ensign, three sergeants, three corporals and two drummers.

Sir John died on 12 May 1689, aged fifty-five. He passed on the estate he had managed successfully to restore to its prime, to his heirs. He had been notably generous in his lifetime but had not fully thought through his intended generosity when he wrote his will. He left annuities to his children which eventually led to the break-up of the Reresby estate.

It was traditional to make bequests to various beneficiaries but an annuity is a constantly dripping commitment from the resources which meant less money would be available for necessary maintenance of property and running costs. John's son, Sir William, resisted the will, contending that as eldest son he should inherit everything and his six brothers

Figure 3.38. Sign of the *Reresby Arms*, Denaby Main
Figure 3.39. The *'Reresby'* has now been changed to the *Milestone* public house.

and sisters should make their own arrangements, although he would help them. As well as the property, Sir John left £6,000 in bonds and cash. William did continue to pay annuities for several years following his father's death but the terms of the will became more difficult to maintain and family feuds ensued. Some of the brothers and sisters resorted to law to protect their interests.

William was not noted for his management skills but was noted for his love of gambling, wagering large stakes. Eventually he lost his estate, pledged against the accumulated debts brought about by his own folly.

Not quite all was lost. Sir John may not have been as misguided as some thought. He may have understood his son's weakness better than he was given credit for and may have feared for the future of the estate in William's hands. He had purposefully split off his Mexborough properties and given them to his second son, Tamworth, and thus saved a portion of his heritage which might otherwise also have been lost by William.

Figure 3.40. St Leonard's Church at Thrybergh. *Brian Elliott*

The *Reresby Arms* (now *The Milestone*) was named after Sir John in honour of the work he did in Denaby Main where he owned property (Figures 3.38-39).

Sir John's memorial is on the north wall of the nave of St Leonard's (Figure 3.40), opposite the door. The inscription (translated from the Latin) is as follows

> *Here are placed the remains of the renowned John Reresby, Baron, the pride and glory of his famous and ancient line, who*

under their Majesties, Charles II and James II to whom he had been most loyal, performed functions both civil, Justice of the Peace of the County, Burgess in Parliament for York City, and Military, viz...Vice Commander of a Squadron of Infantry, Cavalry and Musketry. Governor of the City of York and Bridlington, Colonel of Militia under Henry, Duke of Newcastle, died 12th May 1689. To whose memory his splendid wife Frances who bore him 5 Sons and 4 Daughters in her will left the erection of this monument and next to whom she is buried. Died 11th May 1699.

WENTWORTH, HOLY TRINITY CHURCH
William Henry Lawrence Peter, 8th Earl Fitzwilliam 1910-1948, killed in a plane crash along with Lady Kathleen Hartington (nee Kennedy)

William (Figure 3.41) succeeded as the 8th Earl Fitzwilliam on the death of his father in 1943 (Figure 3.42). He was born on 31 December 1910, at the family home in Grosvenor Square, London. Most of his time, however, was spent on the estate at Wentworth Woodhouse (Figure 3.43). He was very interested in estate business and took great delight in mixing with the local people and estate workers. He was anxious to develop the estate, but not at the expense of the tenants. He had a passion for sport, loved cricket and often took part in local games. It was not unusual for him to arrange for matches to be played on the eleven-acre lawn at the front of the house at Wentworth. He was also keen on fox-hunting, being master of the Derwent Fox hounds from 1943-1947. Like his predecessors, he was a horseracing enthusiast, was Steward of the Jockey Club and officiated at the regular May meetings at Doncaster racecourse. He was active, too, in the Sitwell Park Golf Club and the Rotherham Town Cricket Club.

Figure 3.41. Invitation to Viscount Milton's 21st birthday celebration, 31 December 1931.

The family connections were such that Fitzwilliam managed to persuade the then Prince of Wales (later King Edward VIII) to visit

Figure 3.42. Roasting of the ox, part of the 'Coming of Age' celebrations in Wentworth village.

the Rotherham Boys' Club of which he was chairman. He was also in active support of Rotherham Hospital.

When the Second World War broke out the Earl joined the armed forces. He saw action at sea as well as on land and was awarded the Distinguished Service Cross for his involvement in a blockade against German shipping which was set up from Sweden to England. He served with a special force under Sir George Binney and was one of Sir George's chief officers. He also spent time as a captain in the Grenadier Guards and saw service in the Middle East.

On 19 April 1933, he was married at St Patrick's Cathedral,

Figure 3.43. Wentworth Woodhouse.

Figure 3.44. John F. Kennedy, US President. His sister, Kathleen was killed along with Earl Fitzwilliam in the 1948 air crash. She is buried at Edensor, on the Chatsworth estate of the Devonshires.

Dublin, to Miss Olive Dorothea Plunkett. She was the only daughter of the Right Reverend Dr Plunkett, former Bishop of Meath. The couple had a daughter, Lady Anne Juliet Dorothea Maud Fitzwilliam, who was born in 1935.

Cracks started to appear in the marriage and the Earl's life turned to drink. At a society gathering the Earl was introduced to Lady Hartington, heir to the Duke of Devonshire's estate at Chatsworth. The Marquis was killed during the war. Fitzwilliam began seeing Lady Hartington secretly on a regular basis and they started planning a future together (before she married, Lady Hartington was Kathleen Kennedy, sister of John F. Kennedy (Figure 3.44) who was to become 35th President of the United States and who was assassinated on 22 November 1963).

In May 1948 Lady Hartington's father, on a European tour, was in the South of France. The Earl rented a plane from Skyways Ltd for two or three days with a crew of two, Captain Townsend and radio officer A.F. Freeman. He had decided to meet Mr Kennedy senior to seek his permission to marry his daughter after his divorce from Lady Fitwilliam had been finalised. They flew into a violent thunderstorm west of Valence in France and the plane crashed, killing all on board (Figure 3.45). A 'Vast Concourse' of mourners attended the Earl's funeral before his burial at Holy Trinity Church, Wentworth (Figures 3.46-47). He left an estate of £711,704 on which duties of £11,432 were paid.

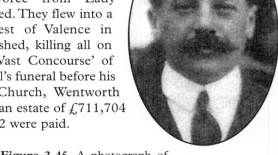

Figure 3.45. A photograph of the Earl taken shortly before his death.

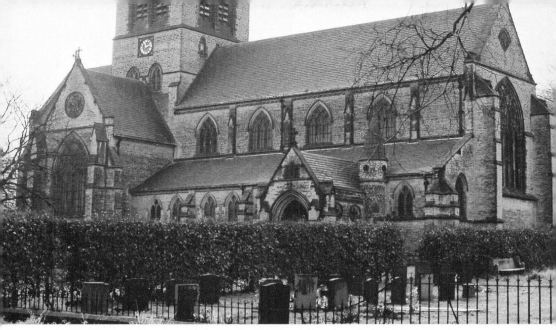

Figure 3.46. Holy Trinity Church, Wentworth was built as a memorial to the 5th Earl who died in 1857. This magnificent building, described by Pevsner as 'A very fine, scholarly piece of Gothic revival' was completed to the design of J.L. Pearson from 1875 to 1877. *Brian Elliott*

Figure 3.47. News headline relating to the Earl's funeral at Wentworth

EARL'S VILLAGE - FUNERAL

Vast Concourse of Mourners

STRIKING MANIFESTATION OF DISTRICT'S REGARD

Begrimed, helmeted miners, straight from the pit bottom, mingled with frock coated and silk hatted mourners in the thousands who thronged the mourning village of Wentworth to pay a farewell tribute at the funeral of Peter, the eighth Earl Fitzwilliam, and last son in direct line who was buried at Wentworth on Wednesday in the shadow of the Parish Church. Lord Fitzwilliam was killed when his private charter aeroplane crashed over France on Friday last, Kathleen, Lady Hartington, daughter of Mr.

SPORTING INTERESTS.
Sporting representatives included Mr. F. Baker (Newmarket), Mr. J. H. Payne and Mr. S. Neal (Rockingham Stud Co., Newmarket), Mr. W. Easterby (also representing Capt. Fielding, Mr. Matthew Peacock and Mr. Harry Peacock, Middleham, Mr. McElligott (British Bloodstock Association), Major Gordon Foster (Yorkshire Committee), Mr. A. Wood (Rotherham Town Cricket Club), Mr. G. B. Needham, captain, Mrs. R. H. Fairburn, ladies' captain, Mrs. W. E. Laughton, ladies' secretary, Mr. R. Edghill and Mr. A. A. Davis (Sitwell Park Golf Club), Messrs. H. Whittaker,

WENTWORTH OLD CHURCH

Richard Marris d.1635, Steward to Thomas Wentworth, 1st Earl of Strafford

Visitors having access to Wentworth Old Church are understandably drawn to the magnificent family monuments of the Wentworths, in particular to the life-like monument to Thomas Wentworth (1593-1641, Figure 3.48), Charles I's chief minister, created Earl of Strafford by a grateful monarch in 1640 but subsequently executed.

THOMAS WENTWORTH
of Strafforde Viscount Wentworth, Baron Wentworth
ntworth Woodhouse, Newmarsh, Querney, and Raby
senetenant of Ireland Lord President of the North

Figure 3.48. The magnificent memorial to Thomas Wentworth, Earl of Stafford. *Brian Elliott*

On entry to the church most visitors will probably walk over the gravestone of a less famous but key local figure, that of Richard Marris who served as Wentworth's steward.

When reading the Earl's papers it is clear that 'his lordship' and 'his man' had a good working relationship. Being a steward of such a large estate demanded many skills, a great deal of time and considerable travel, usually on horseback. It appears that Marris was not immune from taking a drink or two whilst 'on duty', a fact of which the Earl was undoubtedly aware. On one occasion the Earl wrote to him, in the third person, suggesting that his steward mend his ways:

I hear a principal servant of mine has been in a house in Rotherham and become so drunk his clothes caught fire and his friends had to pull him away...
The Earle wishes he could alter his ways.

Unfortunately Marris died, probably from exposure, after falling from his horse on a journey from Ledston to Wentworth in 1635. The extent of his sobriety was not known. The inscription on Marris's gravestone (Figure 3.49) reads

ANNO DOM 1667
[BY] APPOINTMENT OF [THE]
EARLE OF STAFFORD [THIS]
STONE IS LAID OVER [THE BODY]
OF MR RICHARD MARRIS
WHO DIED IN YE YEAR 1635
BEING STEWARD & ANTIENT
SERVANT TO HIS LD EVER
MOST HONOURED FATHER
THOMAS EARLE OF
STAFFORDE

Figure 3.49. The gravestone of Richard Marris, inside the Old Church at Wentworth. *Brian Elliott*

Hannah Jennet d.1765, housekeeper at Wentworth Woodhouse

Being in charge of an enormous household was a post of considerable responsibility. Hannah Jennet's gravestone (Figure 3.50) now rests against the church wall. Referred to as 'Mrs' in the burial registers, she was clearly an individual of some social standing among the estate community of Wentworth. The logistics

Figure 3.50. Gravestone of Hannah Jennet. *Brian Elliott*

of, for example, looking after a household that during twenty weeks might consume 588 pounds of beef and 260 pounds of mutton must have been immense. In addition there was the supervision of everyday tasks such as cleaning, polishing, laundering and so on. Servants also travelled with the family wherever they went.

IV THE SHEFFIELD AREA

In the S. or Shrewsbury chapel (of St Peter's Church) are
some remarkable monuments: (1) the effigies of the founder,
George, 4th Earl of Shrewsbury, and his two wives...; these
are under the arch dividing the chapel from the presbytery,
they are exceedingly fine and in excellent preservation; (2) a
plain tomb, bearing the arms of George, 6th Earl of
Shrewsbury, and his first wife;(3) the 6th Earl's own
monument, against the S. wall. He is the Earl who for so many
years was the gaoler of Mary Queen of Scots.

From: *A Key to English Antiquities: with special reference to the Sheffield and Rotherham District* by Ella S. Armitage (Sheffield,1897)

Figure 4.1. Fine alabaster monument commemorating the 4th Earl of Shrewsbury and his two wives (c1538). *Brian Elliott*

ATTERCLIFFE, HILL TOP CHAPEL
Benjamin Huntsman 1704-1776, inventor of crucible steel

Benjamin was the third son born to Quaker parents from Epworth, Lincolnshire, on 14 June 1704. It is believed that the family descended from Dutch settlers who came to England in 1625 to help drain the Isle of Axholme. At the age of fourteen Benjamin was apprenticed to a local clockmaker. He served his time and by 1725 was working as a clockmaker in the town of Doncaster. Four years later he married Elizabeth Haigh, an Anglican, of Doncaster. They had two children, Elizabeth (b. 1730) and William (b.1733). The marriage does not appear to have been successful, probably because of the pressures put upon the couple by their differing religious backgrounds with respect to raising their children. Huntsman married again, to Agnes Haigh, a kinswoman of his first wife, despite criticism from the Quaker community.

Huntsman's business as a clockmaker flourished and he was appointed to look after the town clock at Butcher Cross in 1727 and the new town clock in 1735. He was renting premises in High Street, Doncaster, and within two years had raised sufficient funds to buy the property.

Figure 4.2. Now *The Britannia*, behind and above the modern front extension is Huntsman's house. *Brian Elliott*

He used to experiment in making tools for clockmaking but found that the quality of steel used in springs, pendulums and other parts of clocks was of poor quality. After some trials Benjamin found that he could melt raw steel in a crucible and alter its constituents to make a more uniform material. Up to then steel had never been developed in a molten state. It had been produced in a bizarre process involving a cementation furnace, charcoal and layers of iron bars and sand - plus several days in time. These problems were not easy to solve and experiments took time.

Benjamin moved to a cottage in Handsworth, near Sheffield, in 1742 and after nine years, in 1751, as a result of the success of his methods, he was able to retire from clockmaking and establish himself as a steel-maker in premises on the east side of Leeds Road, Attercliffe (and later Worksop Road). He was now able to melt and cast steel and open up vast possibilities for development for everyday use. Latterly he lived in a house now known as the *Britannia Inn*. A blue plaque commemorates his residence here (Figures 4.2-4.4)

Huntsman's steel making prospered. From his foundry he was producing steel bars, sheets and rolls.

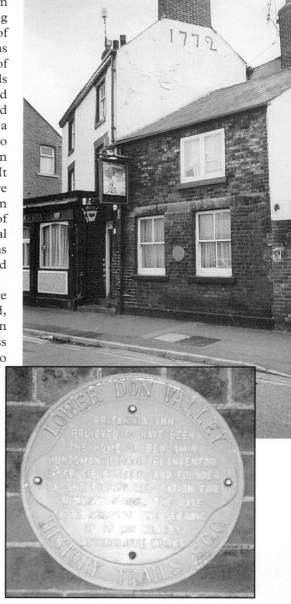

Figure 4.3. On one of the gables of *The Britannia* the date '1772' is clearly visible, believed to be made from pieces of Huntsman steel.

Figure 4.4. Blue plaque commemorating Huntsman's house.

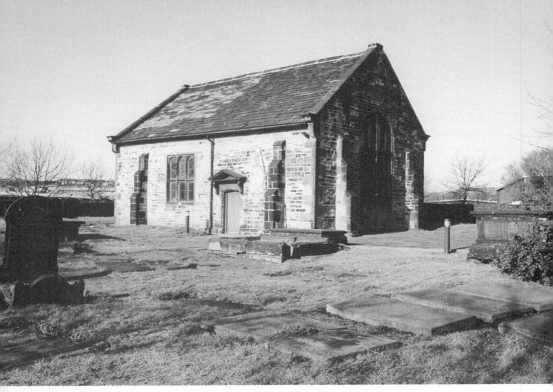

Figure 4.5. The medieval Hill Top Chapel was re-established in the 1630s by leading Puritans Stephen Bright of Carbrook Hall and William Spencer of Attercliffe Hall. The building was reduced to its present dimensions in 1909. The burial ground contains a number of Sheffield industrial pioneers and business entrepreneurs. *Brian Elliott*

Figure 4.6. Benjamin Huntsman's family tomb, with the Hill Top Chapel in the background. *Brian Elliott*

He was a true industrial pioneer and of international importance. He died, aged seventy-two, on 20 June 1776. The Huntsman family tombstone can be seen in the Hill Top Chapel Cemetery at Attercliffe (Figures 4.5-4.6). Restored some years ago, it displays a modern plaque in tribute to the great innovator.

BRADFIELD, ST NICHOLAS' CHURCHYARD

Before Victorian times the church at Bradfield (Figure 4.7) was a chapel of ease within the huge parish of Ecclesfield. It was built on a prominent site, quite near the spectacular motte-and-bailey earthwork known as Bailey Hill.

The churchyard contains many interesting gravestones (Figures

Figure 4.7. St Nicholas' Church at High Bradfield. *Brian Elliott*

Figures 4.8 and 4.9. The surname Elliott was a common family name in the Bradfield area. There are numerous 'Elliott' gravestones in the churchyard. Here are two nineteenth-century examples. *Brian Elliott*

Figure 4.10. The watch tower at Bradfield churchyard.

4.8-4.9), with unusually clear inscriptions, a few dating as far back as the seventeenth century.

An eighteenth century Gothic gatehouse (Figure 4.10) was built here, guarding the entrance to the churchyard. The gruesome practice of body-snatching was rife in some parts of South Yorkshire, Bradfield's deterrent serving as a watch tower against the 'resurrectionist' men. The *Anatomy Act* of 1829 put an end to the 'body trade'.

ECCLESFIELD, ST MARY'S CHURCHYARD

The fabric of the church (Figure 4.11) dates from 1480-1520 , in a Perpendicular 'style'. However, much of the interior owes a great deal to the High Church movement of Victorian times, particularly during the extraordinary incumbency of Dr Alfred Gatty whose wife,

Figure 4.11.
St Mary's Church,
Ecclesfield. *Brian Elliott*

Figure 4.12.
Cover of *Jan of the Windmill* by Juliana Horatia Ewing, 1891. *Brian Elliott*

Margaret (nee Scott) and daughter, Juliana Ewing, were famous writers of children's stories (Figure 4.12). Gatty was vicar for sixty-three years, wrote on Sheffield history and has left us a description of the parish: *A Life in One Living* (1884). Margaret was a published authority on such diverse subjects as seaweeds, zoophytes and sundials. Reverend Gatty's curate, Jonathan Eastwood, even published a parish history in 1862. The vicarage (Figure 4.13) was thus a thriving literary centre.

The large churchyard contains a good variety of many interesting memorials. Like those at St Mary's, Bradfield, most tombstones are in very good condition and a few reach back to the seventeenth century (4.14).

Of the later examples, an unusual inscription can be seen relating to a local field sportsman who never

Figure 4.13. The Vicarage, Ecclesfield, from an Edwardian postcard.

practised on the Lord's Day:

> *In memory of*
> *the Ecclesfield Huntsman,*
> *Thomas Ridge,*
> *who died 13th January 1871*
> *aged 77 years.*
> *Thought fond of sport,*
> *devoted to the chase,*
> *and with his fellow hunters*
> *first in place, he always kept the*
> *Lords appointed day,*
> *never from Church or*
> *Sunday School away,*
> *and his body lies*
> *beneath the sod,*
> *his soul relying*
> *on the love of God.*

Ridge's gravestone can be seen by passing through the main gate, up the steps, and located on the right side.

Figure 4.14. Gravestone of Jeremiah Lord, 1676. *Brian Elliott*

Alexander John Scott MD 1813-1903, Chaplain to Lord Nelson

After Nelson had been killed at the Battle of Trafalgar (Figures 4.15-17) his body was brought back and laid in state at Greenwich. Alexander Scott sat up night after night by Nelson's coffin, greeting all who came to see him. Scott was with Nelson when he died and witnessed the horrors of the cockpit. He saw men dying about him in scores. For three agonising hours he remained by the dying admiral's side. In a letter home, Scott stated that he detested the victory for it had deprived him of his beloved and adored friend:

> '*I will grieve for one I dearly loved and with the greatest affection, and I may now add without the world accusing me of vanity for one who loved me*'.

Figure 4.15. Admiral Nelson.

Scott's grave (Figures 4.18-19) can be located by following the path from the church towards the vicarage. The tombstone is opposite the lamp, the inscription as follows:

Waiting for the redemption of our body, helie buried, Alexander John Scott DD, Vicar of Catterick and south Minster and Chaplain to Admiral Lord Nelson on board HMS Victory *at Trafalgar. He died July 24th 1840 aged 72 years, also his daughter Margaret, the beloved Wife of Alfred Gatty DD, born 18th April 1813, died 20th January 1903, Vicar of Ecclesfield for 63 years and sub Dean of York. Lord I have loved the habitation of thy house and the place where honour dwelleth.*

Figure 4.16. HMS *Victory.*

Figure 4.17. The death of Nelson.

Figure 4.18. Alexander Scott's tombstone.
Figure 4.19. Alexander Scott's grave: detail of inscription.

Joseph Rhodes, killed in 1815 after a barefisted fight.

Across from St Mary's stands the *Black Bull Inn* (Figure 4.20). On 11 April 1815, a heated argument broke out between John Boulden and Joseph Rhodes. They were both residents of the village and both labourers. The fight broke out with a vengeance when the landlord intervened and hustled the contestants in the street. The two men stripped to the waist and were soon surrounded by a crowd. A bare knuckle bout began and continued for, what seemed like, an eternity.

Both men fought for their lives. Eventually Joseph Rhodes fell

Figure 4.20. *The Black Bull* Inn, Ecclesfield today.

before the vicious battery of Boulden's fists and could not get up. He was carried home with severe internal injuries where he died on Friday 28 April.

The coroner's inquest heard Ecclesfield surgeon David Sadly's evidence that Rhodes had died as a result of 'mortal bruises'. The village constable, William Foster, was ordered by the court to arrest John Boulden and charge him with feloniously killing Rhodes. A warrant was issued to this effect signed by twenty 'good and lawful men of the town' and neighbourhood. The constable duly carried out the order.

The warrant also bound over David Sadly, the surgeon, a Mr Johnson and his daughter (as witnesses) and surgeon James Wilkinson of Rotherham the sum of £40 to appear before the jury at York Assizes. John Boulden was conveyed to the gaol of York Castle to await the hearing which took place on 18 July 1815.

After a long trial, during which the charge of murder was reduced, John Boulden, aged thirty-two, was found guilty of manslaughter. He was fined one shilling, to be paid to William Carfirth, the High Sheriff.

Because the charge was reduced, the prosecution was ordered to pay the costs of the hearing, to the sum of £32 13s, including legal costs of £8 13s. The Ecclesfield constables were paid 7s 6d. per day for attending and the two surgeons £1 1s. each. The expenses paid by the court to the witnesses for travelling to and from Rotherham amounted to £6 6s.

Reverend Joseph Hunter 1783-1861, historian

Joseph (Figure 4.21)was born in Sheffield on 6 February 1783, the son of Michael Hunter, a cutler by trade. Unfortunately his parents died early, leaving Joseph to be brought up by Joseph Evans who was the Presbyterian minister at the Upper Chapel in Sheffield. Evans was a scholar with a good library. He attended school at Attercliffe where a classical curriculum would have been taught. He soon demonstrated his interest in historical matters by transcribing monumental inscriptions and other records he could find. His adopted father sent him to the Manchester Presbyterian College, York where he was trained for the ministry by Reverend Charles Wellbeloved.

Figure 4.21. Reverend Joseph Hunter.

In 1809 Joseph Hunter was appointed minister to the Presbyterian congregation of Trimm Street Chapel, Bath, taking his antiquarian notes with him. He soon helped to found the Bath Literary and Scientific Institution and was encouraged to continue his antiquarian pursuits by Sir Richard Colt Hoare (1758-1838), the owner of Stourhead.

Shortly after his marriage to Mary Hayward in 1815, the Hunters moved to Sheffield, Joseph accepting a lesser role as lay preacher so that he could pursue his historical studies. In 1819 his *Hallamshire, The History and Topography of the Parish of Sheffield in the County of York with Historical and descriptive Notices of the Parishes of Ecclesfield, Hansworth, Treeton, and Whiston, and the Chapelry of Bradfield*

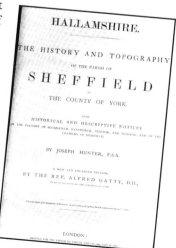

Figure 4.22. Title page from Hunter's *Hallamshire*.

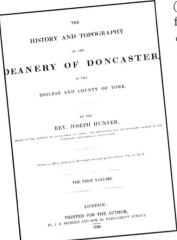

THE
HISTORY AND TOPOGRAPHY
OF THE
DEANERY OF DONCASTER,
IN THE
DIOCESE AND COUNTY OF YORK.

BY THE
REV. JOSEPH HUNTER,

THE FIRST VOLUME.

LONDON:
PRINTED FOR THE AUTHOR,
BY J. B. NICHOLS AND SON, 25, PARLIAMENT STREET.
1828.

Figure 4.23. Title page from Hunter's *South Yorkshire* (vol. 1).

(Figure 4.22) was published and this was followed in 1828 by *The History and Topography of the Deanery of Doncaster in the County of York* (Figure 4.23), the first of two monumental volumes that earned him great recognition as a historian. In 1833 he was appointed as one of the sub-commissioners of the Public Records in London and five years later became assistant Keeper, First Class, in the new Public Records Office, with a remit to sort the immense manuscripts in the Tower of London.

Other important publications followed, including *The Life of Sir Thomas More by his Great-Grandson Cresacre More* (1828), *A Hallamshire Glossary* (1829), an edition of *The Diary of Ralph Thoresby* (1830) and *English Monastic Libraries* (1831).

Hunter returned to the Sheffield area whenever he could, walking round Ecclesfield churchyard and examining inscriptions, even selecting his own place of burial.

He died in London on 9 May 1861 but his body was conveyed to Ecclesfield, according to his own instructions, and interred in his chosen spot under the willows on 15 May.

Sir Henry Ellis, librarian of the British Museum, referred to Hunter in his memoirs and to the strength of his opinions. He related the story of an occasion when the two men were walking in the Strand discussing a doubtful date. Arm in arm they were crossing the street to Somerset House when Hunter became so intent on making his point that he was oblivious to the clattering hooves of the horse-drawn traffic. He gripped Sir Henry firmly and stopped in the middle of the road. They narrowly escaped being run over by an omnibus.

SHEFFIELD CATHEDRAL, ST PETER AND ST PAUL

The medieval parish church was raised to the rank of a cathedral in 1914 (Figure 4.24). From 1936 the old building was incorporated into a new, larger cathedral designed by Sir Charles

Figure 4.24. Sheffield Cathedral, a mixture of late medieval and modern architecture.

Nicholson but his project was abandoned in 1961, replaced by a new scheme, completed a few years later. It is now a modern cathedral with links to a long history. The earliest surviving parts date back to the fifteenth century and in the sixteenth century George, the 4th Earl of Shrewsbury and Lord of the Manor of Sheffield, added the (Shrewsbury) chapel. Major alterations were made to the parish church during the eighteenth and nineteenth centuries.

George Talbot c1528 - 1591, 6th Earl of Shrewsbury

George was the elder son of Francis Talbot, the 5th Earl. He married 'Bess of Hardwick' in 1568 and was selected by Queen Elizabeth to be keeper of Mary Queen of Scots who remained under his charge, principally at Tutbury, Chatsworth, Sheffield Castle and his hill-top residence, Manor Lodge. Talbot was therefore much trusted by Elizabeth.

Figure 4.25. The spectacular memorial to the 6th Earl of Shrewsbury, against the south wall of the chapel. *Brian Elliott*

George's great memorial (Figures 4.25-27), almost stretching to the roof of the south chapel, serves as an unmistakable reminder of his wealth, power and influence. His funeral was one of the most spectacular ever held in the North of England. On a bitter January night the Earl's cortège slowly advanced towards St Peter's, the long winding procession led by two men carrying black staves, followed by seventy yeomen and grooms and 300 'official' mourners. The Archbishop of York and his entourage were at the rear of the procession. It was estimated that 20,000 people were present, the customary dole being given out to the poorest 8,000.

He was succeeded by his second son, Gilbert Talbot (1552-1616) who married Mary Cavendish, daughter of Bess of Hardwick, who, as we have seen, married his father.

SHEFFIELD GENERAL CEMETERY

Faced with a rapidly expanding population, the burial of the dead was a major problem for our Victorian ancestors. The condition of old churchyard burial grounds was causing serious health concerns as well as being offensive to mourners. In order to try to offset the crisis, nonconformists were allowed to establish their own cemeteries via newly established private concerns. These offered dignified burial but only to those that were able to pay since the companies were run as businesses.

Sheffield's General Cemetery Company was established in 1836, away from the town in what was then described as a 'country' location (Figure 4.28). The Company had capital of £25,000 in the

Figure 4.28. Map showing the site of the General Cemetery.

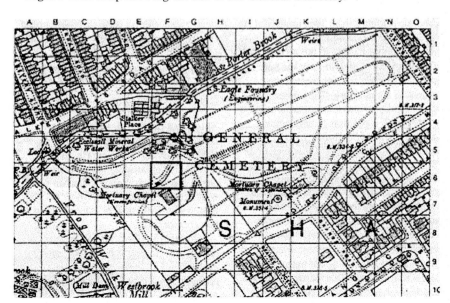

form of a thousand shares. With this sum 'very eligible' land was bought from Mr Henry Wilson, for £1,900. Only a small area – some five acres – was initially set aside for interment since this was thought to be adequate for the city's needs. Much more land was soon in use. Samuel Worth (1779-1870), notable for his design of the Free Writing School (1827) and Cutler's Hall(1832-33), was commissioned to provide a suitable plan and appropriate buildings. He completed the lower entrance to the General Cemetery in 1836. It included an Egyptian gateway on Cemetery Road, the Registrar's house (now used as offices), a nonconformist chapel and the Catacombs (subterranean burial places). At the Ecclesall Road end of the cemetery two obelisks were erected, indicating the beginning of the drive up to the cemetery. It was deemed to be a splendid urban cemetery, where resting places could be adorned with monumental architecture in keeping with the status and wealth of individuals and families.

The *Burial Acts* of 1852-57 resulted in local burial boards being established with a duty to ensure that all people were given a decent burial. The General Cemetery thus contains a wonderful collection of memorials and mausolea.

Samuel Holberry 1814-1842, Chartist Martyr

Holbery was born at Gamston, near Retford on 18 November 1814. Unhappy with life in the army, he bought himself out in 1835 after three years' service. He moved to Sheffield and married Mary from Attercliffe, living at 19 Eyre Lane. Samuel became passionately interested in the rapidly developing Chartist movement and 'The People's Charter' of 1838 with its demands for:

- the vote for all adult males
- election by secret ballot
- equal electoral districts
- abolition of property qualifications for MP's
- MP's to be paid a salary
- annual parliaments, elected every June

In May 1839 a Chartist meeting in Sheffield attracted a crowd of 20,000 but with the Commons' rejection of a National Petition containing 1,250,000 signatures, strikes and insurrection were being considered by the movements leaders. Fearing civil disorder,the one-day strike held in Sheffield on 12 August 1839 resulted in a strong police and military presence. Holberry helped to organise public protest meetings in order to establish the right for people to meet openly and discuss political issues. Some were held in churches and churchyards and there was a large assembly of people in Paradise Square, Sheffield. In September 1839 the authorities reacted by banning any further meetings in the Square but the Chartists continued to organise public gatherings in out-of-town locations.

Nevertheless an illegal public meeting was held in Paradise Square on 11 November 1839, as part of what appears to have been towards a planned attempt at a national uprising. On 12 January 1840, five hundred Chartists were recruited with the object of taking over the Town Hall and the *Tontine Coaching Inn* (Figure 4.29), to be used strategically as 'forts' in the city. The authorities were tipped off by a Rotherham publican the night before the insurrection.

Figure 4.29. The *Tontine Hotel.*

Holberry was arrested at his Attercliffe home, along with his pregnant wife and other Chartist leaders, on the night of 11 January 1840. A large amount of ammunition and firearms was found in the Holberry household.

Holberry was sentenced to four years' imprisonment following his trial at York Assizes. The first few weeks was spent on the treadmill in York Castle prison, followed by months of solitary confinement. Chartists campaigned for Holberry's and his companions' release but he was retained and moved to a hospital wing where he died of TB, aged just twenty-seven, on 21 June 1841. His funeral, held in Sheffield on 27 June, attracted a huge crowd, estimated to be

Figure 4.30. Modern plaque paying tribute to Samuel Holberry.

50,000, along the route to the General Cemetery, with Chartists leaders following the coffin. George Julian Harney, a national Chartist leader, made a political speech at the graveside, re-emphasising the Chartist cause and paying tribute to Samuel Holberry as a Chartist martyr.

A second National Petition, six miles long, containing more than three million signatures, was rejected by the Commons in 1842; and a third (containing numerous forgeries) was thrown out in 1848. But Chartism was the first national movement of working-class political protest and drew the attention of the establishment to some of the injustices of the poor. Between 1858 and 1918 five of the six main points (annual parliaments

Figure 4.31. Samuel Holberry's grave, now leaning slightly to the right.

being the odd one out) of the Charter were partly or wholly achieved; and Samuel Holberry had given 'his life for what he believed to be the true interest of the people of England: a democratic society that would guarantee freedom, equality and security for all (Figure 4.30)'.

Holberry's gravestone (Figure 4.31) can be located by passing through the Egyptian gates, turning left until reaching the railings, then right and taking the first walkway on the right. The grave is reached in about ten yards. The inscription reads:

> *Sacred to the memory of Samuel Holberry who,*
> *at the Early age of 27, died in York Castle after*
> *suffering an imprisonment of two years and*
> *three months - June 21st 1842- for advocating*
> *what to him appeared to be the true interest*
> *of the people of England.*
> *Vanished is the feverish dream of life, the rich*
> *and poor find no distinction here, the great and*
> *lowly end their care and strife, the well-*
> *beloved may have affections but at last, the*
> *oppressor and the slave shall equal stand*
> *before the bar of God. Of him, who life and*
> *hope, and freedom gave, to all through this*
> *vale of tears have trod. Let none then murmur*
> *'gainst the wise decree, that opened the door*
> *and set the captive free. Also of son Samuel*
> *John, who died in his infancy.*

This tablet was erected by his bereft widow.

John Cole 1814-1898, Founder of Cole Brothers Department Store

John, born in Pickering in North Yorkshire, was the eldest of three brothers, namely Thomas (b.1824) and Skelton (b.1827). All three were apprenticed to their father, Thomas Cole, in the drapery business (Figure 4.32). After completing their indentures the brothers gained shop floor experience in Wakefield and Sheffield. John worked in the service of Mr Mark Maughan on Angel Street, Sheffield and also (as did brother Skelton) at Cockaynes. Several letters survive in the John Lewis Partnership Archives from the early period of John's career. One interesting letter in particular, written from Sheffield in March 1837, includes a short description of

Figure 4.32. The Cole family in 1895.
Left to right:: Thomas Skelton 1853-1930; Skelton 1827-1896; Thomas Jnr 1854-1931; John 1814-1898 and **(seated, centre)** Thomas 1824-1902. Taken by G.V. Yates in The City Studio, Davy's Buildings, Fargate, Sheffield.
Courtesy of John Lewis Partnership Archives (ref. 2267/a)

Wakefield and Sheffield and comments on the 'very bad' state of trade in Sheffield. It is also an interesting glimpse of working in a draper's shop at the start of the Victorian era, along with personal observations about 'competitors', religion and health (Figure 4.33).

2267/d(i)

JOHN LEWIS
PARTNERS—P
ARCHIVES

Sheffield,March 21st. 1837.

Dear Parents,

      As I shall have been a month at Sheffield to-morrow I dare
say you will be expecting to hear from me according to my promise and as
I should not like to disappoint you I will be a little within the time.
I proposed. I might have written on my arrival, but knowing that my Uncle
would inform you when I left Wakefield, I was not quite so anxious. I
dare say that you will perceive that I have neglected to attend to the
order you gave me at Wakefield but the reason was that I was not aware
that I should leave so early on the Monday morning which was about 6 o'clock,
but I consider that I left it with one quite as competent for the job as
myself and have no doubt but he will please you quite as well. The day that
I left you proved much more favourable than in the morning, I at all anticipated it being no rain to hurt anything. I thought from the appearance
of the sky between Pickering and Malton that we should have quite a wet
day and that I should be under the necessity of purchasing an umbrella at
Malton, but it cleared up and we had no rain until near York. I was not
five minutes before I was on the other coach for Leeds and when at Leeds
the same just time to get from one coach to the other and arrived at Wakefield
just in time for tea. I need not mention when I left as my Uncle would tell
you that I like Wakefield very well but it is an obscure village in size
compared with Sheffield. I dare say you would be equally surprised with my
selfe to think how all the inhabitants did for a living in so large and
populous a town. The town is situated on an eminence and some of it partly
in a valley. Although I have seen a great deal of it, I have not seen a
fourth part of it nor anything of the kind. Here are a many very beautiful
buildings; I mean public buildings in general as for instance, the cutlers'
hall, the music hall, the cemetery, the collegiate school, the post office,
all of which are built of stone and among others which I could mention. I
walked to the cemetery the first Sunday I was heare. It is a beautiful place
situated on a beautiful eminence, a walk of 2 miles from us; it has not long
been formed consequently there has not been many interred yet; there are vaults
for thousands besides the grass plots. I must proceed with another subject
or this sheet of paper will not contain what I have got to say. As regards
my situation, the trade of Sheffield is very bad at present consequently
business is not so good as it generally is. The trade here seems to be con-
fined to 3 days in the week, Mondays, Tuesdays, and Saturdays. We have not
been particularly busy since I came and I suppose we shall not be likely to
improve soon as the Sheffield folks generally spend up all as they go on,
when trade is good they make excellent wages and might save a great deal
of money but they spend it freely then they particularly want. We are 12
in number at present; I suppose 16 is the full number when trade is good.
I am the woollen man at present. We don't go into the shop until 8 o'clock
in the morning; we are not allowed to go out at nights. We live very well
in general; we get coffee to breakfast, bread and milk to supper with cheese
twice a week. Some of the young men complain very much about their supper
but upon the whole I can do with it very well once a day but the apprentices
get it twice. There is one thing I don't like and that is we get our meals
so irregular and late in general breakfast at 9 o'clock and on Sundays near
10. I suppose we shall be left a good deal to ourselfes soon as the family
will retire to their country house soon which is about 3 miles off and then
a good deal will depend upon the housekeeper we get as regards comfort. Mr.
Maugham is a man that does not talk much to his young men. Mrs.M -- comes

a good deal into the shop and the young men don't like it in general but
she never interferes with my department at all. She pays as much attention
to business as the governor. We keep bonnets but all the drapers of any
consequence do here. It is a larger shop than that at Driffield and a
large bonnet room behind. It is a very nice front 3 squares of plate glass
in height and in width the same. It is only on a stoole that I can reach
the top in the inside. There are a many beautiful shops besides ours.
Mr. M has been to Manchester since I came. He goes once a month or six
weeks. I must know think of drawing to one end for this time. We attend
church twice on a Sunday. We have four parsons and they most of them preach
extempory. I have not learnt anything of the person Humble told me of
but put the letter into the post. The last and the most important thing
is my health without which everything else is vain. I have been pretty
well since I came except a very severe bowel complaint which I suppose is
partly owing to the change of water but I am much better. Our water is not
near so good as you get. I sometimes wish I had some of yours but in vain.
You must write to me in the course of next week if you can as I am very
anxious to know how you all are, especially my father who was, and I suppose
is yet, poorly but shall antioipate hearing a more favourable account from
the room I have left. You will perceive I do not mention any names therefore my love to you, and to all friends, farewell.

    I remain,

      Your affectionate son,

        J. Cole.

N.B. More particulars on my next letter.

Figure 4.33. Letter from John Cole to his parents, Sheffield, 21 March
1837. *Courtesy of John Lewis Partnership Archives (ref.2267/d(i)*

By 1847 the Cole bothers were in business on their own account, starting with a small shop in Sheffield. The enterprise steadily increased into an emporium of note, in fact the largest drapery concern in Yorkshire within a few decades. By 1892 the little shop had become a stately pile, described in 1898 as 'one of the finest blocks of buildings in Sheffield' (Figure 4.34). John was of course the chief partner and took a prominent part in business affairs, even when in his eighties. Writing about Men of the Period in 1897, a few

Figure 4.34. The Cole Brothers store today.

months before the founder's death, one commentator described how John still ' visited the warehouse daily, taking a keen interest in everything around him,'.

Earlier, when the business converted to a limited company, John Cole was elected as chairman of the board of directors.

Cole's obituarist described his 'quiet and retiring disposition' and 'kindly and genial' nature, in fact someone who was 'greatly esteemed' by all who had contact with the man. He was also a noted benefactor of the City of Sheffield. His two principal but by no means exclusive charitable interests related to long support for hearing impaired persons, helping to found the Sheffield Deaf and Dumb Institute. He was a leading figure in regard to the building of Jessop Hospital for Women, giving continued support as a hospital governor.

A staunch Wesleyan Methodist, John Cole's religious life undoubtedly impacted on his business affairs, along with public and private relationships. He was a somewhat reserved individual, certainly one that did not look for 'publicity' but to his friends and acquaintences 'kind-hearted and jovial.' A keen gardener, John enjoyed horticultural pursuits in his leisure time at Prior Bank. He did not have any children, and the reins of business passed to his surviving brother, Thomas Cole of Park Spring House.

John Cole was buried at the Sheffield General Cemetery on Thursday 19 May 1898, the graveside ceremonies preceded by a packed service at Montgomery Wesleyan chapel:

The service concluded shortly afterwards and the 'Dead March' was played on the organ as the procession in the cemetery formed. The male employees of the firm, with the departmental seniors at their head, walked in front of the hearse, and around the grave was a large number of other workpeople and friends. Mr Cole was buried in the vault in which the bodies of his mother and wife lie. Its sides were clothed with ivy, and the top of the coffin was covered by a floralbank, sent by employees at Farbank.

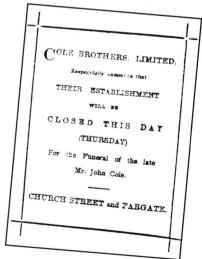

Cole Brothers closed for the day in respect (Figure 4.35). In fact all four hundred employees attended the very well attended funeral when a gentleman said of him, 'Mr Cole was a man in whom I

Figure 4.35. Notice announcing the one-day closure of Cole Brothers for John Cole's funeral.
Courtesy of John Lewis Partnership Archives

Figure 4.36. John Coles' memorial, Sheffield General Cemetery.

found less of what may be called human humbug than any other man I have ever met.'

John Cole's family memorial (Figure 4.36) can be seen by turning left from the main drive, continuing up the path and the grave is located on the right hand side. The inscription reads:

In affectionate remembrance of
Elizabeth, youngest daughter of
Thomas Cole of Pickering,
who died 23rd December 1913,
aged 80 years.
In affectionate remembrance of
Elizabeth, the widow of Thomas
Cole of Pickering,
who died 23rd December 1913,
aged 80 years.
Sacred to the memory of
John Cole of Prior Bank, who
departed this life 15th May
1898, aged 83 years.
So we bringeth them unto the haven
where they would be.
Psalm 107, verse 30.

The present Cole Brothers' departmental store, now part of the John Lewis Partnership, serves as a living reminder to one of Sheffield's most talented but modest business pioneers.

Susan Bielby and daughters - victims of German bombs
The inscription reads

In loving memory of William Henry, dear husband
of Susan Bielby, died 7th March 1940, aged 84
years. Also, the aforesaid Susan Bielby and their
daughters, Emily, Hannah, Millicent Susan and
Anne Bielby, killed by enemy action, 12th
December 1940.

Sheffield Blitz, Nazis Say

IN Berlin early this morning informed German sources stated that large bombing units last night delivered an attack on Sheffield.

This statement followed a night in which German bombers had been active over many areas, especially a Midland town.

A suburban church and a furniture store were destroyed, and damage was done to houses and other buildings.

The furniture store was set alight by incendiary bombs.

Adjoining it is a theatre and the audience had to leave just after a dance band had begun its performance.

They filed out while the band went on playing, and were met at the doors by wardens, who directed them to shelters.

The fire brigade prevented the fire from spreading to the theatre and other property in the block.

CINEMA HIT

Two incendiary bombs fell on a cinema and penetrated the roof, but were extinguished by members of the staff before any other damage had been done.

The film programme was suspended, but the audience was entertained by the manager.

A high-explosive bomb and a number of incendiaries fell on a private housing estate on the outskirts of the town.

Many houses were set on fire, but most of the fires were quickly extinguished.

A tramcar was hit by a fire bomb but nobody was injured.

The church which was destroyed had been hit by fire bombs. Only the shell of the building and the spire were left.

A number of casualties were treated at the hospitals. Some were suffering from shock. One or two from shrapnel wounds. Among them was a fireman.

RESCUED FROM CELLAR

An incendiary bomb which fell in a street of the town was put out by soldiers who were passing.

Two children and their mother were rescued from the cellar of a demolished house, but the grandmother was still buried.

Several public-houses were struck by incendiary bombs, but the fires were soon extinguished.

Other areas over which raiders flew last night included several other Midland towns, Liverpool, North-Western inland districts, an East Anglian town, and towns in the South-West and Wales.

Planes which appeared over a North-Western inland town were met by fierce gunfire, and quickly made off.

This town had its longest continuous 'alert' period for some weeks.

At Liverpool there was no gunfire and no bombs were dropped.

An A.F.S. messenger boy, Robert Cooper, aged 17, put out four incendiary bombs with his steel helmet in a North-East coast town.

FIGHTERS UP

An incendiary bomb set fire to a small chapel at another North-East coast town.

London's alert began early, and heavy gunfire was heard at intervals, but there were no reports of bombs being dropped.

Fighters went up as 'waves of raiders crossed the East Coast at a great height and headed inland.

Heavy anti-aircraft fire met the raiders inland.

Raiders also crossed the South-East coast.

Incendiary bombs were dropped in many of the areas, but they were quickly tackled.

When incendiary bombs were dropped on a North-East town in daylight yesterday the only casualty was a warehouse cat.

Figure 4.37. News report from the *Telegraph & Argus*, following the German raids of 12 December 1940.

The night of 12 December 1940, during the early days of the Second World War, German aircraft bombed the city. Despite the warning of sirens (because there had been numerous false alarms) very few people were apparently disturbed, at least initially. The worst period was between 11.00p.m. and 1.00a.m. when the seven storey *Marples Hotel*, at the High Street/Fitzalen Square junction, was completely destroyed. The night of bombing caused widespread damage and many casualties left the city in a terrible state (Figure 4.37). A further German attack took place three days later. In total, 668 civilians and twenty-five servicemen were killed during air attacks on Sheffield and a further ninety-two persons were classed as 'missing'. In addition, almost 600 citizens were injured. The memorial to the Bielby family is a sad reminder of the personal impact of the 'Sheffield Blitz'. The grave is situated near the nonconformist chapel – enter the cemetery gates and it is found against the wall, to the immediate left.

Thomas Sands 1783-1850, Battle of Waterloo Veteran

To find Thomas' grave (Figure 4.38), enter the cemetery through the main gates, turn right and proceed down the path. Follow the path until you see an opening on the right hand side and Thomas Sands'

Figure 4.38. The grave of Waterloo veteran, Permanent Sergeant Thomas Sands.

Figure 4.39. 1st King's Dragoons Guards. Officer and Trooper wearing overalls.

grave is to the left. The inscription provides us with background information about his distinguished military service (also see Figure 4.39):

> To the memory of
> Permanent Sergeant, Thomas Sands,
> of the Sheffield Squadron of the
> First West Yorkshire Yeoman Cavalry,
> who died 29th March 1850,
> aged 67 years, having served in the
> above regiment, upwards of 22 years.
> He also served 24 years in King's Dragoon
> Guards and highly distinguished himself at
> the very memorable Battle of Waterloo.
> This stone is erected by the non-
> commissioned Officers and Privates the
> Sheffield Squadron
> of First West Yorkshire Yeoman Cavalry.

Mark Firth 1819-1894, steel and armaments manufacturer

Mark Firth, the eldest son of a large family of seven sons and two daughters, was regarded by many of his nineteenth-century contemporaries as the most important of Sheffield's industrialists (Figure 4.40). His father, Thomas (1789-1850), came to Sheffield from Pontefract, and for several years worked for crucible steelmaker Jonathan Marshall at Millsands. Thomas succeeded to the job of head melter at another crucible steel concern, Sanderson Brothers of West Street where he found jobs for his sons, Mark and Thomas.

Mark and Thomas, perhaps because of insufficient wages, set up their own business in 1842, from premises in Charlotte Street, and were soon joined by their father.

The first Firth works was a relatively modest undertaking, occupying just one-third of an acre and consisting of six coke furnaces for melting steel. They had to be 'Jack of all trades' in the early days, unable to employ more than a few hands. The accounts of 1844 show that the average annual income was £73 13s 10d, with expenditures of £70 10s 10d, hardly a great deal of profit for capital investment. Mark was then receiving just £1 15s in wages per week. However, two years later matters had improved so much that Firths were employing thirty men and boys. More importantly, the high skills evident enabled the firm to continue to develop an excellent reputation for quality. Joseph Bridon, another highly skilled melter, came to join them from Sandersons. During the early years Mark Firth used a great deal of energy in promoting and marketing the firm. He gained orders by visiting Birmingham and other places and even established a link with America, including Samuel Colt, the famous US arms manufacturer and the Collins Axe Company of Connecticut.

Figure 4.40. Mark Firth, who contributed so much to making Sheffield 'Steel City'.

By 1852 Firths had outgrown their Charlotte Street works, transferring their steelmaking operations to new premises in Savile Street, next to sawmakers Spear & Jackson, on land leased from the Duke of Norfolk. The new factory was named 'The Norfolk Works' (Figure 4.41).

Figure 4.41. The Norfolk Works, from an advertisement of c1862. The date '1840' relates to the 'foundation' when Thomas and his sons set up in business in much smaller premises.

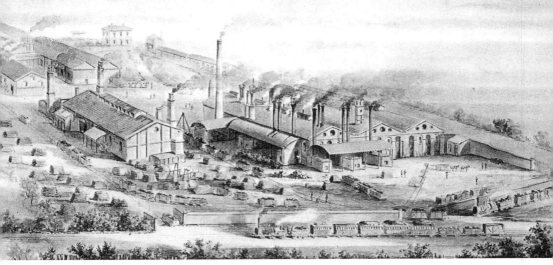

Figure 4.42. The new works at Whittington, near Chesterfield in c1870. It specialised in 'puddled steel' from furnaces marked in this view by numerous small chimneys. The nearby railway was clearly a vital locational requirement.

The death of Thomas Firth Snr, two years Earlier, in 1850, meant that business responsibility lay with Mark and his brothers John, Edward and Charles but Mark was regarded as 'the ruling master spirit'. Land for further expansion was purchased at Whittington, Chester-field, supplying armour to Whitworths, Armstrong's and the Woolwich Arsenal (Figure 4.42). Diversification resulted in the manufacture of iron jib cranes, roof struts, and even railway carriages (for the Indian Railway Company). Opportunistically, a wire drawing works was also established, producing steel wire for the latest women's fashion craze – crinoline skirts.

In 1860 Firths were concentrating on the armaments side of their business, specialising in producing the world's biggest steel blocks, used for powerful guns. The first example had been forged by Firths in 1852 at Clay Wheel's Forge, Wadsley Bridge. Two huge Nasmyth hammers were installed in 1857 and used to forge guns for Armstrongs and Whitworths.

The Norfolk Works were extended in 1863 and two twenty-five ton hammers were installed, with the capacity of making even larger weapons. The noise from these monsters caused nearby buildings to shake and claims for vibration damage from rival firms.

By 1871 Firths launched the famous Woolwich Infant Gun, weighing thirty-five tons and involving the teaming of a thousand crucibles of steel. Two years later a massive eighty-ton gun was cast. The company was also producing steel barrels for the Enfield rifle.

Along with Vickers, Firths were the leading producers of crucible steel, employing over one thousand men and by 1871 a turnover approaching half a million pounds.

Mark did not neglect public offices. He was a councillor for St Peter's Ward (1860-63), Vice President of Sheffield School Board (to 1874) and from 1867 was elected Master Cutler for three years in succession, a remarkable achievement. In 1874 he served as both Alderman and Mayor. When the Prince and Princess of Wales paid a royal visit to Sheffield in 1875 it was Mark Firth who hosted the event. Mark also opened and presented to the town Firth Park, a thirty-six acre estate he had acquired for £29,000.

Mark Firth lived at Oakbrook, Ranmoor, a fine stone mansion with a magnificent tower set within twenty-six acres of parkland. After the death of his wife (Sarah Bingham, daughter of a Sheffield scissors manufacturer), he remarried in 1857, to Caroline, the elder daughter of Thomas Bradley, the Alderman of Nottingham. He had become the wealthiest Sheffield citizen by the 1860s and became a noted benefactor. He opened Firth College (Figure 4.43) at the

Figure 4.43. Firth College (now Firth Court), the forerunner of the University of Sheffield. *Brian Elliott*

Figure 4.44. Firth's Almshouses at Hanging Water.

Figure 4.45. The Norfolk Works of Thomas Firth & Sons c1900. Note the cementation furnaces.

Figure 4.46. Firths Iron Yard c1900.

corner of Leopold Street, the precursor of
the University of Sheffield and opened
thirty-six alms houses at a cost of
£30,000 (Figure 4.44).

Mark Firth suffered a stroke on 16
November 1880 whilst visiting the
Norfolk Works. He was returned to
Oakbrook but never regained
consciousness, dying on 28 November.

Local newspapers edged their editions
in black and even *The Times* devoted a
major section to his death. The funeral
cortege stretched two miles. His will,
proved at £600,000, excluding his landed
interests, property and shares,
demonstrated his great wealth which was
bequeathed to his widow, who died in
1894.

After Mark's death the firm was
incorporated as Thomas Firth & Sons

Figure 4.47. Mark Firth's memorial, General
Cemetery, Sheffield.

IN LOVING MEMORY OF
THOMAS WILLIAM WARD JP
BORN MAY 12TH 1853
DIED FEBRUARY 3RD 1926
AND OF MARY SOPHIA
HIS WIFE,
BORN AUGUST 2ND 1853,
DIED DECEMBER 26TH 1955.
WHO SHALL ASCEND UNTO THE

Figure 4.48. The distinctive grave of Thomas W. Ward.

Figure 4.49. Detail showing part of the memorial inscription.

Limited (Figures 4.45-4.46), still under family control but not dominated by one man.

The tomb (Figure 4.47) of Mark Firth, decked with red forged railings has the inscription:

*In memory of Mark Firth,
born 25th April 1819, died
28th November 1894.
Also Caroline gedling, wife
of the above,
born 12th March 1833,
died 13th July 1894.*

CROOKES CEMETERY
Thomas W. Ward 1853-1926, industrial pioneer: from local scrap metal to international high quality engineering.

The memorial to Thomas William Ward JP , like the man himself, stands out from the crowd (Figures 4.48-49). From very humble beginnings he founded a firm that continues –

Figure 4.50. The one-roomed office in Norfolk Street where, in 1878, Thomas Ward set up in business.

as T.W. Ward Machinery Ltd – to flourish despite the massive industrial changes of recent decades.

An 'appreciation' by his son, Alan B. Ward, provides us with an interesting insight into one of Sheffield's more underrated business entrepreneurs.

Thomas started work at the age of thirteen at the water-powered Walkley Bank Tilt, Rivelin Valley. His employment was dependent on the allocated time that each of the twenty forges had to draw water.

Figure 4.51. Lizzie the elephant must have been an amazing sight on the streets of Sheffield.

Figure 4.52. Thomas W. Ward.

In practice this meant working early and very long hours, from four in the morning until four in the afternoon.

By 1878, now aged twenty-five, Thomas set up in business on his own account, as a Coal and Coke Merchant, borrowing a few hundred pounds as capital from an aunt. Not only did Thomas repay the debt with interest, but told his aunt, in recognition of her trust, that she would receive sums of money from him for the rest of her life.

Thomas' first office was at 39, Norfolk Street, a small second floor room (Figure 4.50). When visiting small cutlers, he realised that there might be a market for the waste steel plates that were abandoned in their yards. He therefore invented and patented a hydraulic press (known as the Ward-Lash Press following improvement by a Mr Lash), which crushed the scrap into bundles which were easily transported for reprocessing at the foundries. Working as a 'Scrap Merchant' his business improved each year. He employed two younger brothers, Joseph and Arthur, and worked long hours in order to develop the trade.

In 1882 Thomas Ward and his brothers moved their business to larger premises in the Corn Exchange and six years later he built the Albion Works in Savile Street, still in use as the company headquarters.

Thomas became wealthy as a result of his enterprise but at the same time contributed to the economy of Sheffield as a whole.

When dray horses were requisitioned during the First World War, Thomas W. Ward used an elephant christened Lizzie (Figure 4.51), undoubtedly an eye-catching sight in Sheffield, and one that promoted the firm.

In his will, Thomas William Ward (Figure 4.52) requested burial in Crookes Cemetery 'under a tree overlooking the Rivelin Valley'. This was an appropriate lofty location for a man who towered over many of his contemporaries due to his opportunism and enterprise and from where he faced the valley where he worked so long and hard as a boy.

Figure 4.53. Contrasting monuments at Dore. *Brian Elliott*

DORE VILLAGE GREEN
Contrasting memorials

Perhaps a fitting conclusion to this 'survey' is a glimpse at two contrasting memorials at Dore village green. On the right can be seen a fine First World War memorial, one of many of course that can be found in South Yorkshire villages (Figure 4.53). On the left a plaque attached to a sandstone monument is inscribed with a dragon and the words

> *KING ECGBERT OF WESSEX LED*
> *HIS ARMY TO DORE IN THE YEAR*
> *AD 899 AGAINST KING EANRED*
> *OF NORTHUMBRIA*
> *BY WHOSE SUBMISSION*
> *KING ECGBERT*
> *BECAME FIRST OVERLORD*
> *OF ALL ENGLAND*

More than a thousand years separate the two events, commemorated by memorials on the ancient border that once divided the kingdom of Northumbria from Wessex.

Sources and Select Bibliography

Aspects of Barnsley, volumes 1-5, B. Elliott (ed), 1993-98
Barnsley's Sporting Heroes, A. Storey, 1997
A Pictorial Record of Mining in Barnsley, J. Threlkeld, 1987
Pits 2. A Pictorial History of Mining, J. Threlkeld, 1989
Aspects of Doncaster, volumes 1-2, B. Elliott (ed), 1997-99
Aspects of Rotherham, volumes 1-3, M. Jones (ed), 1995-98
Aspects of Sheffield, volumes 1-2, M. Jones (ed), 1997-99
Sheffield Steel, K.C. Barrowclough, 1976
Giants of Sheffield Steel, G.Tweedale, 1986
The Making of Barnsley, B. Elliott, 1998
Victorian Rotherham, A. Munford,1989
Rotherham: A Pictorial History, A. Munford, 1994
A History of Sheffield, D. Hey, 1998
A Popular History of Sheffield, J. Vickers, 1992 edition
Discovering South Yorkshire, B. Elliott, 1998
The Making of South Yorkshire, D. Hey, 1979
The History of South Yorkshire Glass, D. Ashurst,n.d. (1992)
A Guide to the Industrial History of South Yorkshire, D. Bayliss, 1995
Yorkshire: The West Riding (Buildings of England series), N.Pevsner, 1967 (revised edition by E. Radcliffe)
Yorkshire West Riding (The King's England series), A. Mee, 1969 (revised edition by F. Beckwith Jr.)
The History and Antiquities of Doncaster, E. Miller,1804
Hallamshire. The History and Topography of the Parish of Sheffield, J. Hunter, 1819 (see also enlarged edition by Rev. A.Gatty, 1869)
South Yorkshire. The History and Topography of the Deanery of Doncaster, volumes 1-2, 1828-31
St George's Church at Doncaster, J.E. Jackson
The Coronation History of the Barnsley British Co-operative Society, 1862-1902, anon.,1903
Railway History of Denaby and Cadeby Collieries, A.J. Booth
The First Black Footballer, P. Vasili, 1998
Thomas W. Ward 1853-1926, A.B. Ward, 1973
Bag Muck Strike at Denaby Main, J.C. McFarlane
A Mexborough Scrapbook, B. Chambers

We Will Remember Them. An Anthology of South Yorkshire - Local History and Events, G.Brearley & G.Oliver, n.d. (c1995)
Roy Kilner: Somewhere He is Smiling Now, M. Pope
Wentworth. A Brief History, volume 2, G. Hobson
Cycling is My Life, T. Simpson
Historical Notices of Rotherham, J. Guest
Chronicle of the Twentieth Century, D. Mercer (ed), 1990 edition
A Biographical Dictionary of English Architects 1660-1840, H.M. Colvin, 1954
The Concise Dictionary of National Biography, volumes 1-3, 1993
The West Riding of Yorkshire, J.E. Morris,1911
Churchyards of England and Wales, B. Bailey, 1987
Discovering Famous Graves, L.F. Pearson, 1998
Sheffield & Rotherham Independent
Sheffield Telegraph & Argus
Barnsley Chronicle
South Yorkshire Times
Doncaster Gazette
Ivanhoe Review (Rotherham Library)

INDEX OF PEOPLE